TAKING
T H E
RISK
...MEET YOUR FATHER

DR. ALPHONSO EVANS SR.

Taking the Risk…Meet Your Father
By Dr. Alphonso Evans Sr.

I would like to take the opportunity to thank God for allowing me to overcome my fear of addressing the absence of my father and giving me a platform that encourages others.

I would like to thank my beautiful and awesome wife for believing in me when I doubted my purpose in moving forward with this project. Your support is always consistent! Love you!

I would like to thank my children for being the reminder I needed to be vulnerable during the project!

I would like to thank my mother for allowing me to be authentic in the process even when I knew it was sometimes difficult. You Rock!

I would like to thank a Great Brother for giving me some "gems" that I still carry through this life's journey of being a black man in America.

I would like to thank the most inspiring group of men for contributing to this project with their time, guidance and most of all stories. You made the purpose greater and gave the platform a "bigger reach"!

Thank you to Reverend Dr. Alyn E. Waller(My Pastor) and my Enon Family!

Thank you to Bishop David G. Evans and the Bethany Baptist Church!

Thank you to Bishop Keith W. Reed Sr. and the Sharon Baptist Church!

Thank you Gregory A. R. Love!

Thank you Bryan Dearry!

Thank you Brendon J. Jobs!

Thank you James E. Harris!

Thank you Reginald A. Day!

Thank you Yvesmark Chery!

Thank you Bennie L. Ruth!

Thank you to Bakari Sellers for your kind words and support!

Thank you Kingdom Exposure Printing!

Thank you GBD Gallagher Business Development!

Thank you Myzie Media!

Thank you to all of the panelists, panel participants and to everyone who supported along the way! I appreciate you!

Now Take the Risk and share these powerful stories to your family, friends, co-workers,and church members!

Thank you!

TAKING THE RISK... MEET YOUR FATHER
ENGAGE, CONNECT, AFFIRM, TRANSEND & UNDERSTAND

CONTENTS

INTRODUCTION

Engage, Affirm, Transend and Understand

Growing up, some family, neighbors and friends frequently made comments regarding my grandfather's alcoholism and my mother's addiction to drugs. Yes, it always hurt, but it also motivated me to ensure my life would not just be another statistic of a Black boy from North Philadelphia, who did not know his father and had an absentee mother.

Let me begin by introducing myself, I am Dr. Alphonso Evans, Sr. As a child, I grew up with a drug addicted mother, an absentee father and raised by aging grandparents. I always believed God wanted me to overcome these obstacles, find my true purpose and transcend my circumstances. When I was young, I was helpless against the negative words spoken about my family, but I always had full control of my actions. The challenges I faced inspired me to do more, be more. Had it not been for these hurdles, I doubt I would be where I am today, sharing this dialogue with the world, authoring books, and reminding everyone of the importance of understanding the father-son relationship.

There was a time when I did not want to face the reality of my story. I felt extraordinary shame but now, as a grown man, I realize my story could not only free me but potentially free others who have walked a path like mine. At each stage in life, God places us on assignment. I believe the vulnerability and transparency of sharing my pain and triumph with others is my current assignment. Something larger than me decided that these hardships were never meant to break me but prepare me for this very moment of liberation.

I began this journey simply wanting to find my father, but through the building of relationships and conversations with other inspiring Black men, I found so much more. I embraced the opportunity to speak with other men who, in some cases, would break down, sobbing as they shared stories about their relationships with their fathers. Some of these men smiled as they reflected on fond memories of their father. Sadly, others found these conversations to be extraordinarily difficult, as they had intentionally suppressed this pain for years. This book is the compilation of stories and experiences of 11 successful Black men and their relationships with their fathers. Some stories will make you laugh, some will make you smile, others will make you cry, but all will encourage you to reflect on your own relationship (or lack thereof) with your father.

Although father-son relationships provide the foundation of this book, you will also read about so many of the unsung heroes; the strength, perseverance, and resilience of mothers, grandmothers, and aunts…the women who kept so many of these boys, now men, afloat. This reminds us that none of our stories are complete without the recognition of the women who played such integral, life-influencing roles. Some stories will highlight the sacrifices women made to help their sons maintain a strong relationship with their fathers. Others will demonstrate the pain they had to personally overcome while also helping their sons "grieve" the loss of their fathers. Regardless, all will show the strong love and support these women provided for each of these men.

This book reveals raw emotions serving as a platform to engage, affirm, transcend, and understand the multifaceted dynamics of fatherhood, the essential role women play, and the power of a second chance. Throughout the book, these 11 men begin to divulge a myriad of emotions, reflecting on their childhood, often expressing the desire to have an opportunity to at least speak with their fathers once again. These men reflected on fathering their own children and how their past influenced their relationships today.

Taking the Risk Meet Your Father, is a true labor of love. It began as a personal journey but has intertwined with the journey of others. Like so many, I still look to fill the void of not knowing my father and pray I am eventually provided the moment to close the wound that has been open almost all my life. If my father is no longer alive, I know I will need to accept the finality of the journey.

I pray this book serves as part of the healing process for those who feel insurmountable pain as well as a constant reminder to those who have had healthy relationships with their fathers to pay it forward. The stories to follow surpass the stereotypical idea that fatherhood is a monolithic experience rather than a mosaic with significant disparities. Every relationship has the potential to grow, love and change.

CHAPTER 1

—*Dr. Alphonso Evans, Sr.*
"I still needed to know my story, to hear for myself
"why he didn't want me."

The Heavy Weight

For years, I have been working internally to build the courage to search for my father. A father that, at best, was only the blurry memory of a six-year-old boy. At 27, I vividly recall the unquenching desire to search for my father. At that point in my life, I was preparing to marry the love of my life and felt it could not be a more perfect time to explore my true-life story. Up until that moment, I experienced many milestones but as I embarked on marriage, I could not shake the feeling of wanting to find my father and understand my story. I drove to Philadelphia's City Hall to try to secure valid information to "jump start" my journey. Unfortunately, it yielded nothing and at that very moment, I knew if it was my intent to learn more about the identity of my father, I would have to gain the emotional strength to ask my mother. I dreaded even the thought of the conversation.

To be honest, I am not sure what I expected as a response from my mother, but I chose to express to her my desire to find my father before approaching my "big day" with my future wife. Even though I imagined how she might react, I still found myself crushed by her chilling four-word response, "You need some help!" I understood that response to mean, "Why would you want to meet him?" While this was clearly my mother's perspective, I still needed to know my story, to hear for myself "why he didn't want me", why I was not a priority and why he never chose to come back. While I did not want to hear anything but an opportunity of support, I now understand that my mother's response was deeper than I could ever imagine. I knew I had to regroup and dismiss this idea out of my head, I mean who was I kidding with this "courage"? Disappointed and saddened, I decided to suppress my desire to seek answers and concluded that the journey I longed for would just not come into fruition. For years to follow, I found myself blocking out my insatiable desire for answers to ensure the comfort of my mother. However, many years later, thirteen to be exact, on the cusp of my 40th birthday, I began to feel another major event in my life come with the absence of my father with the weight becoming heavier with each passing day.

The Backdrop

My mother was born and raised in North Philadelphia. From early on, she demonstrated great defiance and rebellion against my grandparents who struggled to tame her "strong willed" spirit. Ultimately, my mother's uncontrollable disposition led to her attraction to a man ten years her senior. While she was a young and impressionable high school student, he was a 26-year-old man. In 1977, my mother, who attended a Philadelphia Catholic High School, became a pregnant teen out of wedlock. At that time, being 16 and pregnant left a young girl feeling ostracized and criticized by family, friends, and the community. Typically, the teenager was banished from their home and sent to stay with family down South, pressured to terminate the pregnancy or relegated to a group home for pregnant teens until the child was born.

My grandfather was both devastated and enraged his daughter became pregnant as a teenager. My mother faced family and friends showing their disappointment, especially after they learned that my biological father had not taken advantage of her and that it was consensual. They often questioned her future and whether she planned to bring the pregnancy to term. My mother, true to form, told the world she would be keeping her baby, unphased by negative responses. Due to my mother's age, the age of my biological father and the circumstances surrounding her early pregnancy, my grandparents immediately became my guardians. When I was born, my mother was 16 years old and my father was 26 years old. I am not too certain of the extent of their relationship and, to this day, have minimal details surrounding my biological father. From what little I understand, my father may have been married during the time he and my mother had their brief encounters. I also believe I have half-siblings and extended family I have never met.

Many children have heard the glamorous love stories of their parents and the excitement surrounding the birth of their children. I knew no such story. My mother lived in a group home until I was born. My father's name was on my birth certificate, but I am not sure if that is his actual name, due to the amount of difficulty I have had locating him. I have been told that he has always resided in the same city and has family in the very neighborhood I grew up in, so the difficulty of finding him has been very frustrating. Unfortunately, I only know what others have shared with me. I recently learned I was born a stone's throw from where I live today. I suppose in some ways my life has come full circle.

As a child, my mother did not live with my grandparents and me. Although I did not see her daily, she was not what many would consider an absentee mother because she called consistently and checked on my well-being. Many factors influenced my mother living separately from us, including the tension between my mother and my grandmother. Both my mother and grandmother were stubborn and strong willed, making it difficult for them to amicably live together. My grandmother demanded respect without question, something my mother either could not, or would not supply. While I never called my grandmother "mom", she was nothing less than a mom to me. She raised me and was responsible for my daily care. My grandmother was the person who stayed by my side when I was unable to sleep. She sacrificed all she had to ensure I never went without. She made doctor appointments when I fell ill, kept me safe and ultimately gave me what every son wants from a mother, unconditional love. As an adult, I understand how blessed I was to have not one, but two mothers.

Not Biological but Mom and Dad Nonetheless

Biologically, Albert and Beulah Evans were my grandparents but sometimes, it seems a disservice to confine their impact to those words. My grandmother was an independent, strong woman and I undoubtedly recognize that my mother and I both get our strength and perseverance from her. My grandmother was very opinionated, confident in her convictions yet extraordinarily nurturing, a characteristic I consider to be a gift. She was born into a large family with 12 siblings. After facing racism and educational barriers, my grandmother and her siblings moved to Philadelphia in search of better opportunities. My grandmother and her siblings were extremely close and served as my village. As a child, I did not understand their impact but looking back, I realize they were the lifeline I never knew I needed.

Compared to my grandmother, my grandfather's upbringing was quite different. The bond my grandfather and his siblings shared was linked to land their parents worked on and left them as an inheritance. They loved each other dearly but were not openly affectionate like my grandmother's family. My grandfather was a functional alcoholic that, somehow, never missed a day of work. Even though he had a fourth-grade education, he was the smartest man I ever knew, and I had such admiration for him. I can remember the consistent lectures about education and the non-negotiable conversations about my attending college. My grandfather was a provider. My grandmother and grandfather had a complicated relationship which frequently became intense and argumentative. However, even throughout the difficult and challenging times, they shared a mutual love, encouraging them to stay the course. My grandparents were married for over forty years, only separated by the passing of my grandmother and later my grandfather. Despite their differences, I never questioned their love for me or each other.

Neither of my grandparents had a quality education, yet they sacrificed and struggled to ensure I received every educational opportunity possible. They were determined to provide me the absolute best, even if it meant they had to do without. I never knew about their finances, but they were adamant that I attend Catholic school from kindergarten to ninth grade. They searched for people in the community with children that were excelling in school to tutor me. I can remember telling my grandmother that I did not need a tutor, as I was a straight A student. My grandmother disagreed, feeling the extra assistance would make up for their inability to help me academically. I did not like it then, but I recognize now that everything they did for me was for my betterment and came from a place of love. These examples do not even begin to fully explain why I feel that the simple words "grandma" and "grandpop" do not do them justice.

Strained Relationship

In my younger years, my mother and I had a relationship that better mirrored siblings than that of a parent and child because she did not live with us. I remember those challenging times because my grandmother and mother were at "war" about me. Once my mother secured housing, she saw an opportunity to raise me full-time, however, my grandmother vehemently opposed the idea. I can remember visiting my mother, but my grandmother always found a way to bring me back home with her. At eight years old, I was aware of my mother falling victim to the crack cocaine epidemic in Philadelphia. It not only affected her life, but it also perpetuated the strain in our parent-child relationship.

My mother's drug abuse caused me to experience significant trauma. The crowd my mother associated herself with could sometimes become violent. I remember one of the most disturbing episodes like it was yesterday. It was a rainy weekend when I heard my mother banging on the front door. As she entered, I could see bruises on her face. My mother ran quickly up the stairs and not far behind was someone forcefully banging on the front door, demanding to enter the house. I was young, naïve, and even though my gut told me something was not right about this person, I opened the door. The person was screaming, trying to push past me to get to my mother. Quickly, I called for my dog, Champ, who jumped and fiercely attacked the unwelcomed "guest" in our home. They immediately backed up, running out of the house. That dog likely saved my mother's life. I believe this event is what solidified my love for dogs.

Even though my mother struggled with her addiction for many years, she remained transparent about the challenges she often faced. Years later, she frequently apologized for the decisions she made because of her drug abuse. I found my mother's honesty and openness to be symbolic of the courage she developed to look me in the eye and share some of her darkest moments. My mother made sure she was the one who told me of her struggles and that I did not hear secondhand stories from others.

When I was a teenager, I began feeling resentment toward my mother. I was in high school and could better identify my feelings of abandonment. However, there was also a layer of guilt, as my mother's feelings were as important to me as my own. Now, as an adult, I realize acknowledging the feeling of abandonment at the hands of my mother was a crucial step in my healing process. I never reminded my mother of her mistakes. There was never a need, as she always understood the pain her decisions caused me. Forgiveness allowed me to grow beyond those painful moments. It was during these times I realized, God had me right where I was meant to be.

The Journey

My father was never really discussed in our house. For my grandparents, they never even uttered his name or acknowledged his existence. However periodically my mother would disclose some descriptive information about my father such as him being a boxer and a public transportation bus operator. I did not understand how my family could pretend that my biological father never existed but that was the reality. As time moved forward, I began to embrace the notion that he never existed as well.

My grandmother and most of her siblings were married and raised their children in two parent households. This was not my reality yet, in many cases, my uncles and older cousins considered me one of their own, taking me under their wings and helping to raise me alongside their children and grandchildren. While no one explicitly said, "we are doing this because your father is not in your life," I often felt like it was an unspoken sentiment. Everyone made sure I was a priority. I never went without something I wanted or needed. My family supplied everything, as if I was a descendent of royalty. When I think back, in addition to love, there was empathy that rooted many of their actions. I am grateful for all they did for me but the reason behind their kindness still stings.

For a period, I believed my mother was only concerned with herself. I felt abandoned. First by my father and then, my mother. For many years, my mother fell victim to her addictions, leaving her far too irresponsible to care for me. Somehow, she would still show up at my grandparents' house to see me, tell me she loved me and that she was proud of my accomplishments. At times when my mother seemed beyond help, it was the positive memories that kept me emotionally afloat. Still, I felt confused, as my mom sent mixed messages. How could my mother love me but still be addicted to drugs? I thought she loved me more. She was always apologizing for her situation and behaviors. Even today, she lives with guilt because of her choices in life, but our relationship has seen more positives than negatives. As an adult, I understand better but as a child the trauma of the reality was heavy. I believe God had a divine plan for her to be the mother she was to me. We both learned important life lessons, persevered, and became stronger people. I will forever honor my mother, embrace, and care for her. I want to model this kindness to my children, so they realize that we all make mistakes, and we all can forgive.

Despite the feelings of abandonment, I was able to forgive. I believe this was a direct result of my relationship with God. My grandmother's sister belonged to Zion Baptist Church and I would attend with her regularly. My grandmother did not attend church but would question if I did not attend Sunday worship. She knew how important it was for me to have that collective fellowship. I have always been deliberate with my relationship with God, which has helped me with the forgiveness I was able to extend to my mother. To me, forgiving others for their words and actions is necessary because I believe this is all part of letting pain go and peacefully moving forward. I have come to learn that life is not always about finding closure, but it is about seeking understanding to allow for new beginnings.

Two Short Encounters

I only recall meeting my father one time. Through my six-year-old eyes, I can remember my mother and father taking me to a local playground. I vaguely recall his brown skin which brought me a sense of comfort because it helped me to understand my balance of melanin since my mother is so fair. As my mother and father talked on the other side of the playground, I recall running by the swings, then each of them coming over to play with me. This was a great day for my family, and I anticipated it would serve as the beginning of many more, but unfortunately that was not the case. That one encounter was the only intentional interactive moment I had with my biological father.

The only other time I can recall seeing him was briefly while walking with my aunt at the intersection of Broad and Erie Ave. I recognized him as the same man who played with me at the playground just a little over a year earlier.

I remember saying to my aunt, "That's my dad."

She said, "Well, go ahead, I am coming."

I ran after my dad as he was walking to the subway. I hollered "Dad! Dad!", but unfortunately, lost sight of him. There was so much disappointment in that moment. When my aunt caught up with me, I said, "He's gone." She looked down at me and said, "That's OK!" But it did not feel ok at all. From that day forward, every time I walked past a subway station in Philadelphia, I remembered running down those stairs. One encounter with my father was intentional and the other by chance, but neither led to what I was yearning for from a father. My relationship with my father was completely non-existent and the hurt that accompanied this abandonment was, and still is, indescribable.

I did not put the pieces together at the time, but now I recognize that, when I painfully watched my father disappear into a crowd of people, my aunt was there to pick up the pieces and serve as the nurturing balance I needed. She may never understand the significance of her presence at that very moment, but I will never forget what she meant to me that day. In hindsight, I am unsure of how that day would have unfolded had anyone else been there with me. She was always there for me, attentive to my needs and did everything she could to help my grandparents raise me. Even after getting married and starting a family of her own, my aunt remained present in my life and I never questioned her love for me. God knew my aunt needed to be the person with me the day I saw my father entering the subway because after such disappointment, only she could have provided the support I needed to ease such heartache. I am forever grateful for all she selflessly did for me.

It was not until I was almost 30 years old did I realize I was harboring deep anger and resentment toward my father. I found myself running a "race for success", not realizing I was only trying to prove to myself that my father's abandonment did not affect me or my success. Now, I realize that being on an achievement fast-track was something I felt I could control, serving as a distraction from that which was out of my control. The effects of abandonment were real, leaving me emotionally insecure and blocking my ability to build relationships with others. I noticed that when I would meet someone, I was initially hesitant to share personal information. This has improved over time and now, when I am comfortable, I make friends for life.

My Schooling Experience

Mr. Clemens, my seventh-grade math teacher, was an educator who made a significant impact in my life. Mr. Clemens was extremely strict. When I would try to give up or when others gave up on me, Mr. Clemens remained. His words encouraged me to work hard. His rigidity was something I needed so desperately in my life. Mr. Clemens showed me that nothing in life was free; I had to work for everything I wanted. So, I had to stay focused in school; he gave me no other choice. The educational experiences of my grandparents were quite negative, and they wanted better for me. The opportunity to concentrate on anything other than school did not exist for me. This was their focus and, by default, became mine. They did not personally have the tools to ensure my academic success, but they made sure supports were in place when I needed help. In the life of a child struggling with parental abandonment issues, it is sometimes the educators who pour into their lives each day that make the difference. Every child needs a champion, and I am grateful that when my grandparents had exhausted everything within their capacity, Mr. Clemens became my champion.

Going to Catholic high school was part of my grandmother's educational protection of me. She refused to allow me to attend the public high school, no matter how much I begged. I attended Catholic high school for ninth grade but due to financial constraints, my grandparents could not afford to keep me there. Finally, I had my opportunity to attend a magnet public school. I applied and was accepted to several high schools, but my grandmother still had the final say and permitted me to attend one specific, small high school. I knew it was the right decision. That moment changed my life.

High school was a wonderful experience, but the difficult decision of college was now upon me, right when my grandmother's health began deteriorating. She had a heart attack, and it seemed her health quickly began to worsen. I knew I needed to be home, so I told my grandfather I wanted to attend a local college so I could help care for my grandmother. I attended my first choice, Temple University and was excited to have the campus experience while also being only 15 minutes away from my grandparents. Temple University was a great fit and provided many opportunities for me to demonstrate my leadership skills. I enjoyed my college experience and became friendly with many of the professors, which made the experience even better. My matriculation and graduation were great accomplishments but would have never come to fruition had it not been for my grandfather. The accomplishment was the dream my grandfather manifested through me and it was important he see this success. I owe him everything.

So Much More Than My Pop-Pop

My grandfather was an amazing role model and by far, the smartest man I knew. He could talk about faith, astrology, politics, the intended purpose of any dog breed, anything! He was clear and concise with his words, so, regardless of age, he was easy to understand. While his formal education stopped at the fourth grade, my grandfather taught himself to read. I always looked up to him and my uncles because each of them showed me nothing but unconditional love. My grandfather would constantly preach to me about the importance of my education, keeping my head in the books and being more successful than him. As a child, my grandparents ensured I was always involved in youth leadership programs, such as at the Boys and Girls Club, The Explorers program and youth leadership programs with the church. Each of these opportunities provided me leadership exposure and helped develop and strengthen my academic skills. Growing up I learned that the man of the house should be the protector, provider, and care for his family at all costs. Now, as an adult, I am most comfortable being a protector and provider.

My grandfather only told me (aloud) he loved me once. I knew of his love by his daily demonstrations of affection, by all he did for me and, remaining by my side when others chose to walk away. I remember it was late one evening, about seven years ago, I was getting ready to leave my grandparent's house. As I was walking out the door my grandfather unexpectedly said, "I'm very proud of you. I love you." I replied, "Thank you. I love you too, Pop, Pop". I cried the entire drive home, as this was such a significant moment in my life. It was only at that moment I realized how much I needed to hear those words from him.

That same night, my grandfather had a fatal heart attack in his sleep. I will never forget hearing my wife's phone ring early the following morning. I heard my mother screaming through the telephone and knew something was wrong. I said nothing but immediately jumped out of bed, grabbed my clothes, and ran out the door. I knew it was about him. I had to see him. I fell down the stairs running out of the house. This was one of those moments where the body has the fight-or-flight response, so I picked myself up and ran to my car. My phone rang and rang, but I could not answer it.

It was too late.

I was too late.

I did not make it in time.

When I arrived at the house, he had already passed. I was devastated. I never had the opportunity to say goodbye to him. But I believe my grandfather knew his time was ending, and I think that was why he finally chose to tell me he loved me. He knew this was going to happen and I would need the reassurance that only he could give me.

While I admired and loved my grandfather, I do not choose to follow in his emotional footsteps. I aim to be a father who openly shares his love with his son. I kiss and hug my son, making sure he knows how much I love and support him. I practice tough love, I am a provider and a protector, but without question, I am also nurturing. I try to guide and steer him in the right direction, helping him make smart decisions. But, most importantly, I practice what I preach and tell my son how much I love him daily.

If I were to pass one lesson down to my son from my grandfather, it would be understanding the importance of knowledge. He showed me that anything was possible. I learned that degrees and money are not everything in life. My grandfather believed that once a person had exposure and access to knowledge, the possibilities were endless. I would like to share these wise words with my son, as his journey is already much different than mine. He is growing up in a house with both of his parents and more opportunities at his immediate disposal.

The Ultimate Sacrifice

I have incredible respect for my grandparents. They put their lives, plans, and dreams on hold just for me. It is not the job of grandparents to raise their grandchildren. But without them, I would have likely been another statistic, so I honor my grandparents for making this ultimate sacrifice. This was not a requirement but a choice. I have watched so many grandparents struggle raising their grandchildren. Sometimes people believe grandparents owe this to them, but my grandparents did not owe this to me or my mother. They freely sacrificed just for me. I never realized the magnitude of their sacrifice until I was older. They were the angels God sent to earth just for me.

Sometimes Second Chances Are All You Need

Through life's journey, I have learned there are some things you can never get back, a chance after it has been wasted, words after they have been spoken, anger after it has been acted upon, tears after they have been shed, the moment after it has passed and life after it is gone. However, sometimes second chances are all you need. My mother saw her second chance as an opportunity to better herself. My mother has celebrated over 25 years of sobriety, continues to serve in the medical field and is looking forward to retirement in a few short years. To say I am proud of her accomplishments is an understatement! Words will never explain my mother's strength, resiliency, transparency, and will. The strong will that caused her to be a defiant teenager is the same will that gave her the determination to win her battle over addiction. Many succumb to their addictions, but my mother's resilience led her to becoming clean and the greatest 25 years of my life. Time is all we have. It cannot move faster or slower. It is important to live in the moment. I am grateful God granted my mother and me a second chance to build our relationship.

My grandparents showed their love through their actions, not their words. My mother was different, always telling me how much she loved me even when she could not care for me as a mother should. One of the greatest gifts my mother gave me was the ability to express my love in words. Today, I easily express my love to my children. For some, the words "I love you" are difficult to say. They were difficult for my grandparents, but I am grateful my mother said them with ease.

Recently, I was able to garner up enough courage to revisit the conversation about my father's whereabouts with my mother. This time, the conversation ended with my mother's blessing. Growing up I heard many fatherless sons say, "I don't need my dad". I also heard many single mothers say, "I was his mother and father". Though my mother never said those words, I could not help but feel my search for my father felt like an act of betrayal to my mother. My mother's blessing was the encouragement and support I needed to intentionally pursue this journey without reservation.

The Void Is Real

I believe every child who does not have a parent in their life has a major void, but especially a son not having a father. I believe every black boy should know their father. I have heard stories of parents who do not share the identity of their father with their children to protect them. In my experience, I have found that this "secrecy" is not uncommon, especially for black women who often bear the responsibility of raising a child on their own. I no longer want this to be my reality. I want the truth. My mother was beyond blessed because she had my grandparents to pick up her broken pieces. Many women are not as fortunate. Honestly, I have questions and I want truthful answers. In my line of work, I encounter children everyday who do not know their fathers, or their fathers are not responsible. When I look at those black boys, I see myself, and realize how blessed I was to survive the challenges connected to not having my father in my life.

A Letter to Dad

Dear Dad,

I can vaguely remember your face; however, I will never forget seeing you that one time at the playground and noticing that your skin was so close in color to mine. This was exciting for me because my family was so fair-skinned, and I often wondered the origins of my darker hue. I feel the need to tell you a little bit about myself since our encounters were so brief. I am the only child from my mother and grew up in a large extended family, which served as my village. There are so many family members, neighbors, friends, and teachers who contributed to the man I am today. While there were some rough spots, I ultimately had a great childhood filled with love and opportunities. I do not know if you remember my grandparents, but they provided stability for me throughout my life. Sadly, both are now deceased. As you know, my mother was young when she had me, but we have had the opportunity to grow together and I honor her ability to be resilient when times were difficult. The greatest gift anyone ever gave me was my introduction to Jesus Christ, which I know is the only reason I can write this letter to you.

I had the opportunity to embark on an educational journey, which led me to over 17 years as a principal. Currently, I am an Assistant Superintendent, who now understands my purpose in life, which is to help Black and Brown children, seek, embrace, and secure the greatness that lies within each of them. I married a beautiful woman; she is the brains in the family. I have a phenomenal son and a tremendously awesome daughter, who I hope will have an opportunity to meet you one day. They have inquired about their grandfather. I have been honest with them and they are aware of my desire to locate you. I always thought you would ring the doorbell one day, especially since I knew you were aware of where we lived. Even though that day never came, and I always wondered why you did not want me, I forgive you. It took me a long time to get to this point but as a grown man, I am seeking understanding rather than blame. For the last 16 years, I have been looking for you to no avail. However, I feel I am closer than ever. My prayer is that one day I will be able to look you in the face and through watery eyes see a reflection of less disappointments, more hope, and new beginnings. While I do not know who you are as a human being, man, and father I still carry you with me every day and believe that our latter can be greater than our past.

Love Your Son,

Alphonso Evans Sr.

CHAPTER 2

—Gregory A. R. Love
"My dad loved me more than anything and always
made sure I knew it... I miss him so very much."

Who Am I?

My name is Gregory Love. I grew up in a small town in southern, New Jersey. My father was an entrepreneur, and my mother was a nurse. My father's family were close. I grew up around my grandmother, aunts, uncles and many cousins. Everyone loved my dad. We are still a close-knit family.

Background

From what I understand, I was a pleasant baby. I was quiet and raised as an only child but have two half-sisters, Jill, and Charmaine, from my father's previous relationships. They have been inspirational in my life and I can truthfully say my Dad loved and spoiled us equally.

My Parents Love Story

My mother is from Georgia and my father, New Jersey. My parents met while my father was receiving treatment for an injured back. He had a history of back issues. When my father was young, sports recruiters were looking to draft him to become a semi-pro baseball player. He was so talented; teams were looking to draft him right out of high school! Unfortunately, a string of bad luck stopped my father from achieving his dreams. During one particular baseball game, my father was sliding into home plate and broke his ankle. Not long after that, he was then involved in a horrific car accident, causing considerable injuries to his back. My father was devastated. His career as a baseball player was over even before it began.

Since my father was no longer able to pursue his career as a professional athlete, he found a career in the trucking business. He owned and operated a trucking company. However, much like baseball, another severe back injury landed him back in the hospital. While in the hospital, he met my mother who was a nurse. My father was in the hospital for quite some time, giving him many opportunities to get to know my mother. My mother arrived at work at 6:30am each morning and as she prepared for her shift, my father would watch her. He did this every day for almost two months! My mother showed no interest in him, saying he was "fresh" and "too old." My mother's co-workers noticed and teased her, but my mother did not waiver. This did not dissuade my father. He began to pursue my mother. He would ask her co-workers to send my mother to his room so they could talk. My dad was persistent, and he wore my mother down and she agreed to go out with him.

My parents had their first date in Atlantic City where they strolled the boardwalk and got to know each other outside of the walls of the hospital. At the end of the evening, my mother went to the restroom to freshen up. She was so embarrassed when she noticed her hair was standing straight up on the top of her head! When she came out of the restroom, she asked my dad, "why didn't you tell me my hair was standing all over my head"? My dad said, "I thought you knew" and they both started laughing! My parents began dating and after five years of a loving courtship, I was conceived. They married when I was four years old. I was the ringbearer at their wedding, which was small and intimate with the closest members of our family. What began as an intense pursuit, turned into a lifelong devotion. My parents were together for almost forty years, until death, them, did part.

Music

My musical journey started at age four. My grandmother, who played the piano and organ would sit me on her lap when she played. She brought me my first little keyboard. My parents eventually noticed that I had musical talent. I was taking private piano lessons before I even entered kindergarten. Unfortunately, my first piano teacher and I had a rocky start as she expressed to my parents I would never excel as a musician because, I, "could not keep still long enough to learn." Instead of letting that discourage me, my mother and father found a different piano teacher, Mr. Donald W. T. Cary. We immediately, "clicked" and I continued piano lessons with him until high school. He was not only my teacher but my mentor. He helped prepare me for my entrance audition at Morehouse College and sat in the audience for my senior recital when I graduated with my Bachelor of Arts Degree.

Every Friday, my father would drive me to my piano lesson. That was our special day. Mr. Cary was tough, and many students would leave his studio in tears. He had a long wooden stick and if you played the wrong notes, he would hit your hands. I jumped each time that stick hit my hands, but his training taught me discipline. I hated the idea of my hands hit so I made sure to practice at home between lessons. I wanted to be ready for Friday. Mr. Cary quickly became my "Musical Father," as he taught me discipline and perseverance. There was a poster on his wall that he often quoted. It said, "Shape up, or ship out!" He would quote that poster almost every piano lesson, especially if the playing was not to his liking. My father always said that he felt conflicted because he was proud that Mr. Cary was my musical mentor but unhappy with his disciplinary methods.

Fridays with Dad

My dad loved me more than anything and always made sure I knew it. Every Friday, after piano lessons, he would take me out to my favorite restaurants. This was always exciting; just him and me. This tradition started when I was young, with choices like McDonalds, and Burger King. As I matured, so did our restaurant choices. We went to more expensive restaurants, steak houses, and waterfront properties. My father used this opportunity to not only groom me with knowledge and life-skills for business, finance, and family, but to also show me new and exciting places to eat for when I started courting and finding love for myself. He wanted me to know how to impress a date. I would love to start a similar tradition with my own son. He is eighteen months now, but as he grows, I want to continue this legacy. These opportunities and experiences were profound in making me the man I am today.

My father and I would talk about a range of subjects, including my college choices, life goals and dreams, friends, and relationships. Supplying wisdom along the way, I remember him telling me that if I were to go into business, it was important for me to know how to do every job within my company. He never wanted anyone to threaten the success of my business if they decided to quit. He often reminded me of the importance of building strong, honest relationships. Many of his business referrals developed from his building of meaningful relationships and friendships. He used to tell me, "When you don't know what to do, do nothing." I did not understand what this meant until I was older but now, I realize this simple statement was profound. During challenging times, my father's philosophy guides my decisions. My father always believed in the importance of consistency, grit, and relationship building. My father was a stickler for focus and discipline. His favorite place for building relationships was Dunkin Donuts. He loved to have coffee and donuts early in the morning with his friends. It was his morning ritual after finishing his night shift.

A "Man's Man"

My dad was a "Man's Man". He was an athlete. He played baseball, basketball, and football. He was exceptional in baseball and was going to the semi-pros until his accident and ankle injury. I know he was distraught, and it had to be an emotional battle within to have to accept the reality that his dream was now unachievable. Growing up, he taught me some of his baseball secrets. He bought me my first glove and baseball. We used to go to the Phillies games to watch the pros play. I enjoyed playing the sport but not like my father. I played first base and the outfield. I remember making the All-Star games and my father getting so upset with the coaches…and this was little league. My dad loved his sports!

My dad made friends effortlessly and found it easy to get to know anyone who crossed his path. He was warm, supportive, and kind. My father would give you the shirt off his back. Even now, years later, people stop me to tell me about my father's impact. He was there to offer advice and mentored others in the community. It's one thing to know the impact your father has on your life but to understand the impact your father had on the lives of so many others is an unexplainable feeling of joy and pride.

The Entrepreneur

After accepting the harsh reality of not becoming a professional athlete, my father began to consider a venture into entrepreneurship. He had a keen business sense and decided to open an antique furniture store. Unfortunately, the business did not take off as he hoped, so he closed the store and started a trucking company. Like the furniture business, his trucking business was unsuccessful. Still motivated, my father started a janitorial company. This was where my father found success, for more than three decades. The company was able to secure many janitorial contracts and my father found his niche. Through his many friendships, he was able to find suitable employees to work for his company.

At that time, in the mid 1980's, my father was the first black man to have office space on Broad Street, in Woodbury, New Jersey, an upper-class, white, privileged neighborhood. This was a considerable accomplishment, as no other African Americans had offices on Broad Street. He was admired, well respected and, successful. He had many trucks for his cleaning business and forty employees working for him. With no more than a high school diploma, he shocked many with his success.

Education

After graduating high school, my father attended trade school. After only completing a few courses, he dropped out. He had a high school diploma and a handful of trade school/college credits. My father came from a family of entrepreneurs and felt that was his calling. His brothers, and uncles were construction builders, electricians, plumbers, and tradesmen, who enjoyed building homes and businesses. There were also other businesses within my family such as, catering, day-care, job placement, and other trucking companies. I guess my father couldn't escape becoming an entrepreneur, it was in the family blood.

I referred to my father as the "human calculator". He had a way with numbers which helped boost his business success. I would quiz my father, rattling off equations he could solve faster than a calculator. Our home church noticed his aptitude for numbers and appointed him the vice-chairman of the trustee board. He sat in that position for many years, handling the church's finances. To this day, I have never seen anyone manage numbers like my father. My father was a numerical force as he calculated his employees' payroll, ensured our church was financially sound and managed our home finances.

A Sheltered Childhood

When I was young, my parents tried to shelter me from the drug activity occurring in our town. Many of the problems occurred on the local basketball court which was challenging for my parents as they were trying to strike a balance with me playing sports while also protecting me from the bad influences in our neighborhood. They exposed me to every sport except football. My mother did not want me playing contact sports. She and my dad had many conversations about this (she won!). I played basketball, baseball, ran track and field, and swam on the Olympic swim team.

I fostered a few friendships while playing sports but found closer friendships with some of the guys in my immediate neighborhood. My neighborhood friends at that time were Joey, Wayne, and Lamar. I envied Lamar because he had a go-cart when everyone else had bicycles. I begged my parents for a go-cart, but they refused for fear I might have a horrific accident while driving around with my friends. Overall, I had a sheltered, controlled childhood. My friends were "wholesome and respectable" and my parents felt comfortable inviting them into our home. I was active in school taking part in many after school programs, groups, clubs, and sports. I now realize that those experiences created the balance I needed, influencing the person I am today.

Dad vs. Mom

As a child, I was more attached to my mother. I was a mama's boy, and, to a certain extent, still am today. I think it has a lot to do with my father and mother not getting married until I was almost five-years-old. They seemed to have a very lengthy engagement. This is in part due to life events and getting to know each other better, because there was a fifteen-year difference in their ages. I spent most of my early years with my mother.

After my father and mother were married, my father worked night shifts. Because he owned a janitorial business, he would have to clean and manage his employees overnight while businesses were closed. I remember one of his biggest accounts was the Del-Monte Fruit plant where many of my father's employees cleaned overnight. My mother would get me up in the morning, fix me breakfast and get me ready for school. When I came home from school, they would switch, and my father would be home to watch me. This worked for my parents and I rarely had to have a babysitter because of their opposite work schedules.

Favorite Children

In my humblest opinion, I believe my father's favorite child was his second daughter, Charmaine. She always had a special place in my father's heart. I used to be amazed at how easy it was for her to get my dad to give her money. I never minded their bond because I had a similar bond with my mother. Even though I was raised as an only child, my sisters and I would argue like siblings. My dad made sure we all had cars when we attended high school and college. My sister, who was the middle child, had three Nissan Maximas, yes, three! She destroyed two of the three cars. Her driving skills took some time to evolve. I had a Plymouth, Breeze in high school and bought a BMW when I graduated from college. My father financed my sister's cars and my first car, but my mother and I bought my car. I guess we eventually evened out the rivalry.

Unfortunately, my oldest sister, Jill, was not around much. She and my father had a disagreement when she was young, and she began to build her life with her biological mother and stepfather. This hurt my father tremendously as he was always the kind of man that wanted to take care of all his children. He saved money for Jill to go to college and she did not accept it. When Jill got married, she did not ask my father to walk her down the aisle. Even though that was Jill's wish, I think she regrets it today. As a boy, I remember sitting in church on Jill's wedding day watching my father cry as Jill walked down the aisle with her mother and grandmother. At the time, I remember not understanding the circumstances but I had a heightened awareness of my dad's pain. My father made countless attempts to make amends with my sister. Repeatedly, she refused to reconcile. Jill harbors so much anger, she even refused to attend my father's funeral. She is the one who lost out on our father's love. How sad for her.

Dad's Health Decline

During my matriculation at Morehouse College, my mother informed me that my father was having health issues again. What my father thought was his lower back causing him pain again, we later found out was cancer. Consequently, this caused him to work less due to the constant pain and discomfort. As the Chief Executive Officer of his company, he could take time off, but with a lower salary. Being that it was around my sophomore year in college, this concerned all of us because I still had to finish my undergraduate degree at Morehouse. At that time, tuition with room and board and miscellaneous expenses was around $35,000 a year.

As a result of my father's decline, my mother began to work two jobs and I also landed a job playing the piano and directing a choir for a well-known episcopal church in Atlanta, Georgia. These were not easy years for my father who often made sure everything was taken care of financially. I graduated Morehouse College with a degree in Music and went on to pursue graduate work at Columbia University. Unfortunately, by this time my father was diagnosed with prostate cancer which had turned, unbeknownst to the doctors, into bone cancer, spreading all over his body. I withdrew from my graduate program at Columbia to help my mother take care of my father. This was not an easy decision for me as I struggled with seeing my father's decline.

One day, I remember my father called me on my cell phone because someone had hit him while he was stopped at a traffic light. I immediately knew something was not right as his voice sounded weak and weary. That morning, he was sitting in his sport utility vehicle (SUV) when another man, who was ill, crashed directly into the back of my father's SUV. It seemed that after my Dad's car accident, his health really took a dive. He began frequenting the local hospitals, rehab facilities, and specialist's offices, only to go back again and again; trying to get his health in order.

Dad eventually ended up at home with my mother and her friend who is a nurse. They took very good care of him. Unfortunately, I could tell that these were not easy years for my mother who continued to work full-time and nurse him. I also did the best that I could, helping but privately grieving. I did not like seeing my father like this; bruised-up, and with cancer. Afterall, he was my superhero! I remained quiet, prayerful and somewhat aloof coping with his closing demise.

During this time, before his death in 2016, my father told me that he wanted me to go back to college and finish my master's degree. Well in 2018, I did just that! With the support of Dr. Alphonso Evans informing me of a local graduate program, I was able to finish my master's in education degree, graduating Summa Cum Laude from Gwynedd Mercy University in Gwynedd Valley, Pennsylvania in 2020. I graduated with a 3.97 Grade Point Average. I was also inducted into the Kappa Delta Pi International Honor Society for my achievements.

I am now currently enrolled in the Doctor of Education program at Gwynedd Mercy and look forward to finishing in a few years. I know my father is smiling down from heaven as he always wanted me to finish graduate school and move to higher heights and possibilities. I also want to set a great example for my son, Gabriel, who I hope will one day pursue college and graduate school. When Gabriel is old enough to read this book, I hope that he will be as proud of me as my Dad would have been. I hope that I have set an excellent example for him to follow scholastically. I don't know what our relationship will become, and I know I have big shoes to fill, but I pray that I will be the father to him that my father was to me and even better.

Letter to Dad

Hey, Dad! I miss you so very much. I want to thank you for the time you spent with me. I want to thank you for our weekly restaurant outings and everything you have poured into me. I want to thank you for the sacrifices you made that I knew of and the ones I am still learning about now. I thank you for being someone who was respectable in the community and church and gave me responsibilities along the way, so I too could become an upstanding man like you. Thank you for leaving the blueprint for how I should conduct myself.

I apologize for not being there as much as I should have at the end of your life. When I heard that you were diagnosed with cancer, it was heartbreaking. You had always been full of life, and energy. To see you confined to our house, or rehab centers, was almost too much for me at that time in my life. It hurt me to see you in a way that diminished your spirit, and your physical being. It hurt me to see you deteriorate the way you did in the last two months of your life from cancer.

I love you! I thank you for being an outstanding father, husband, and leader. Thank you for instilling in me the wisdom that you did and touching so many lives along the way. I look forward to passing on some of what you taught me to my son, your grandson, Gabriel, who you never met, but who has so many of your personality traits…already! Thank you, thank you, thank you!

Your Son,

Greg

CHAPTER 3

—Bennie Ruth
"I took the lessons you gave me. I think I became better....
I thank you for forgiving yourself, because I forgive you."

My name is Bennie Ruth. I was born on January 7, 1970, at 8:30am in Savannah, Georgia. Both my mother and my father are from Savannah. Personally, I think I resemble both of my parents however, I have been told quite a bit that I look more like my father. I am a junior and was always proud that my father and I carried the same name. Most people down south have a nickname, and I could not be "BJ" because that is my mother's nickname, short for Burma Jean. So, I became "Bentie" and Bentie has stuck with me throughout my life.

My parents met while doing community work in some of the toughest neighborhoods in Savannah. They distributed flyers, cleaned the neighborhood, and spoke with young children, encouraging them to remain focused and to stay in school. I truly believe history repeats itself. When I retired from the United States Army, I took a job as the Deputy Director for Community Engagement in Philadelphia. It involved a lot of what my parents did such as, community service, mentoring, and talking to children about the importance of staying in school and getting a good education. During my tenure, I conducted one of the largest community cleanup initiatives in the city and primarily focused on community engagement and bringing people together.

My parents' upbringing impacted how I was raised. My mother was raised in a loving household, but my grandfather was abusive at times to my grandmother. They eventually separated, and my mother was raised by my grandmother as a single parent with her six siblings. My father was raised in a very abusive household. My grandfather on my father's side, was very demanding and left little room for error. He was abusive to the entire family including my grandmother, my father, and his two siblings. With this as his example, my father eventually became abusive as well. It was not always this way, my mother told stories of how their relationship was extremely loving, until my father joined the United States Army. He had that old southern mindset that a woman should be barefoot and pregnant. My mother was in high school when he joined the Army. He intentionally cut holes in the condoms to get my mother pregnant. My mother became pregnant with my sister and they married soon after. However, within a year, my father did the same thing, and then I was born. Soon after I was born, my mother, who was not even 18-years-old, was diagnosed with uterine cancer and had to have a hysterectomy. After her surgery, she was unable to have more children.

Even as a young mother and wife, education was always a priority for my mother. This was completely opposite from what my father believed. Each time she attended school, my father would become more abusive. He would fight with her after school, knowing she needed to complete home-work assignments. During one specific incident, my father intentionally went to the school to fight my mother but the principal stopped him. He told my father to leave my mother alone and allow her to get her education. My father refused, but in spite of the ongoing opposition my mother went on to graduate as valedictorian of her class and pursued her college degree at Savannah State University. My father continued his abusive behaviors but the final straw was when he pushed my mother down the stairs with my sister in her arms. She realized at that point that it was too much. She was furious and my father had the audacity to fall asleep as if nothing happened. My mother recalls putting us to bed and grabbing a knife with thoughts of killing him. She says she looked at us and then at him. It was in that moment that she decided not to kill him but to leave. The next morning, my mother told my father she was taking out the trash, but instead, she grabbed my sister and me, all of us in our pajamas and ran a quarter of a mile to my grandmother's house. She explained to my grandmother what happened and told her that she was leaving him. I remember my uncles escorting my mother back to the house to protect her as she collected our belongings. Soon after, my mother filed for divorce and that was the end of our nuclear family.

My mother started a new life and a new career as an educator but struggled because my father refused to financially contribute. However, my mom made sure we always had what we needed. While I did not get everything I wanted, I did get everything I needed and lived in a home filled with happiness and love. My mother was a seamstress and sewed all our clothes through high school. I remember she would sew popular logos on our homemade jeans so they would mimic what was stylish; she worked tirelessly to make sure we were happy. She exuded positivity, was extremely loving but was also demanding. She was serious about us having good manners, high grades, an overall love for God and our family.

A Non-existent Relationship

My mother made continual attempts to stay in contact with my father so my sister and I could have a relationship with him. She always left the lines of communication open so that if one day he came to his senses and wanted to have a relationship with us or at least pay child support, he could. He never did. He never even tried. My relationship with my father was basically non-existent. The next time my mother saw our father, we were in junior high school. She spoke to him about how we were doing and that he should visit us. Every time she saw him, she would say, "I don't want your money, I want you to see your children and you may need them in the future." He reached out and made promises that he would visit us but he never actually kept his word.

Picking up the pieces (Maternal Love)

With my mother having to take on all the responsibility of raising my sister and I, while maintaining a career as a teacher, we spent a lot of time in the projects with my grandmother. She was the matriarch of the family. She would constantly give little jewels of knowledge. As a dark-skinned male, she and my mother would always make sure I knew the importance of being content in my own skin. Once when I was little, I put bleach in the tub just because I did not want to be dark like my dad. My mother freaked out, but my grandmother made sure I was proud to be dark-skinned. She took me to pick berries, she picked the lighter berries and told me to pick the darker berries. She explained "the blacker the berry, the sweeter the juice." She wanted to show me that there was not anything wrong with the darker berries; just like me, I am darker, and I should be proud. It was my grandmother's words and her action that changed my perception of my image. From that day forward I remember being so proud to be a dark-skinned man.

Although my mom made sure that I had what I needed there were a few things she just did not and could not understand about raising a young man. But thank God there was help along the way. My mother involved herself in every aspect of my life, including school, sports, and even dating so she could help me be successful. For example, she had the Superintendent of Sunday School show her how to tie a tie so she could teach me. My mother and grandmother made sure I knew how to cook, clean, and provide for myself. They encouraged me to learn the skills I would need to be independent and if there was a skill I struggled with, we worked on it until I could do it correctly. Both my mother and grand-mother did everything they could to make up for the absence of my father.

I realize that they couldn't fill that void but they tried their best and I would never change any of that.

My childhood was full of love and support but there were times when my father's absence created a void. I remember my friends talking about their fathers and the relationships they had and, in those moments, I would wish my father was around. When I played youth and high school football it was hard to see the other players who had their fathers cheering them on from the sidelines but noticing that my father was not there in the stands. I must admit, I missed my father's cheers. However, I was lucky to have my friends' father, who was also my football coach, cheer for me. He was so much more than a coach. He would provide insight and knowledge about being a young black man and showed me the potential he knew I possessed. This is what people mean when they refer to the village. I am so grateful for the village but that void that my mother, grandmother and the village tried to fill just didn't go away.

One of the most memorable quotes from my childhood is, "You're on the right train by the wrong track… GET ON TRACK!" This was from my favorite teacher, Mr. Olgesby. He was my ninth-grade geometry teacher. Tall, slim brother with a big Afro. He was meek but did not take any mess and was serious about young black men and women and learning math. He really focused on young black men being successful. Every day he would try to teach us life lessons. He would say "If you lay down with dogs, you'll wake up with fleas." Which I interpret as, if you spend time with the wrong people then you will end up like them. Mr. Olgesby always reminded us that if we showed up, worked hard, and stayed on the right track, we would not fail. He made sure to get us ready for college and life. My mother enforced the same expectation at home, college was always at the forefront of our family conversations. Because of my mother's love and success in education, quitting was never an option. My mother made sure my sister and I knew the importance of going to college and with a good education we could accomplish our goals.

Initially, I attended Albany State University in Albany, Georgia and completed two and a half years but due to a personal family event, I decided to leave college and join the U.S. Army. I fell in love with the military, had a wonderful career and remained active for 23 years. My mother always taught us to be leaders, and because of this discipline the structure of the Army was enjoyable. Eventually, I returned to college to pursue my education and graduated with a bachelor's degree in Business Administration and Psychology. Additionally, I have earned three Master's degrees: one in Business Administration with a concentration in Human Resources, a second in Hospital Administration with a concentration in Conflict Resolution and a third in Education. Currently, I am pursuing a Doctorate in Education.

The Call to Reconcile

At one time, I thought that my father was making progress. I missed my dad and wanted him to keep the promises he made to me. I remember the one time he showed up. He picked up my sister and I and took us to get something to eat. We talked about school and our after-school activities. He then took us to his house where he lived with his girlfriend and her children. I remember the house being filthy, there were roaches everywhere, which was the total opposite of our clean and orderly home. My father told us to make a pallet and sleep on the floor. Immediately, my sister said she did not want us sleeping on the floor and asked if there was another place that we could sleep. His girlfriend yelled, "No!" Immediately, my sister called my mother, and we went home. That was the last time my father contacted us.

I did not see or hear from my father for the 15 years to follow. My aunt called to tell us that my father had terminal cancer. My first response was, "So, what does that have to do with me?" But after giving it some thought, I decided to visit him. It was difficult, the cancer had hit him hard. Although he was not present in my life, I remembered what he looked like and this was not the same man. Looking at him, I felt overwhelmed with unmistakable, gut-wrenching emotions. Those feelings of sadness were struggling with those of anger and resentment for abandoning me when I was a child. My family raised me as a child of God, and I understood the forgiveness of Christ. To know the teachings of Christ and to think of my upbringing, I could not, in good faith, abandon my father as he had done me. I knew that because of the lessons my mother and grandmother taught me, I would need to find love and forgiveness in my heart.

Knowing my father was at the end of his life, I changed my entire military career path, and I requested a station transfer to Savannah, so I could care for him. The doctors gave him three months to live. During this time, my father repeatedly apologized for the mistakes he made when I was growing up. He was constantly in pain, both mentally and physically saying, "This is my payback." I would say to him, "That is not how God works." I prayed for him and my response to his guilt was, "Stop apologizing, I have forgiven you for the past, let's start from this point loving each other." We spent every day together connecting and doing the things he wanted to do. We would go to the beach just to talk and forget about his sickness. Every day was different for us. Our relationship blossomed and he finally became my dad. This time showed me how much love he had in his heart and he gave it to me until his last breath.

My sister told me that she also forgave our father. On December 9th, her birthday, she decided she wanted to see him and personally express her feelings of forgiveness to him. We went to the hospital, but we were too late. My father passed before we arrived. My sister was heartbroken that she never got the chance to tell him she forgave him, but in my heart, I am sure he knew.

I miss my dad! I came to love him. I wish he could have met his grandchildren. I make no excuses for his actions, but I know that in our five months together, my heart changed, and the emotional weight disappeared. For so many years, I hated and missed him at the same time. I feel so lucky God blessed me with the opportunity for us to reconcile. Now, I miss him in a way far more painful than I ever expected.

Girl Dad

Ironically, I learned to be a good father based on the mistakes my own father made. I put so much emphasis into being a good father for my children, creating a relationship that is the direct opposite of the one I had with my father. I have been blessed with three daughters. It amazes me that the Lord always puts dynamic women in my life. It was my mother, grandmother, and sister, and now my three daughters; all these women have shaped me into the person I am today. My goal is to leave a legacy for my daughters in the hopes they will live by the example I have shown them.

I always remember a question my youngest daughter asked me that I thought was extremely important. The first time, when she was around 13 years old, and again as a freshman in college. "Dad, would you want me to date a guy like you?" The first time my answer was, "Absolutely not!" Her mother and I had separated, headed for divorce and I was an angry and bitter man. The second time, I said, "Absolutely yes! You should date a guy like me." I understood the changes I needed to make in my life and the importance of building a stronger relationship with God. I often think back to those conversations. They encouraged me to continue to strive to be the man my daughters would want to look up to and a model for the type of man they should look for in a partner.

Mentorship

When I was in the US Army, I mentored many young soldiers. But it was not until I retired from the Army and started working in Philadelphia that I saw the impact mentoring had on the lives and the futures of young men. I volunteered as a mentor with Philadelphia's Department of Human Services Boys Track mentoring program. Three dedicated and powerful men invited me to join the program. I still mentor many young men in the Philadelphia area. It always surprises me that so many young men believe it is somehow a rite of passage to go to prison. No matter how many times I suggest otherwise, these young men make choices that lead them to incarceration. Maybe someone in their family, a father, brother, or an uncle went to prison and they believe this is their only route. This motivated me to encourage many young men to consider college or the military. I challenge them with questions and scenarios to push them to see they have the potential to forge a different path for themselves. I teach them to love themselves, their community, and those around them. I make sure to show them a black male figure that is not afraid to show emotions- especially love.

I want to be the best husband, father, son, and brother. I also want to be the best for my entire community. My goal is for people not to see me as something great in terms of money or success but for my willingness to give back. I want to mentor and show young people that they have the power to be better and give back, helping those less fortunate. Most of my military career was recruiting. That is where my 'bug' for mentorship started. I wanted to help develop young men and women into being better and giving back. I want to be a role model for black youth to show them that together, we can make a difference. I want to make my dad proud.

A Letter to My Father

Dear Dad,

Why did you leave me? Why did you fight my mom when she loved you? Why didn't you stay connected with my sister and me? There was a missing part. Why didn't you visit us? Why did it seem like you did not love us? Why? Why were you not stronger than your father? Why couldn't you take his lessons and be better? I took the lessons you gave me and I know I became a better man.

You had so much knowledge. I thank you for sharing that knowledge the last five months of your life with me. I thank you for apologizing.

I thank you for forgiving yourself because I forgave you. I thank God for everyday of those five months we spent together. Even the times I had to clean you up and take care of you, it gave us an opportunity to reconnect. It gave me opportunities to fall in love with you. It was a blessing that we were able to move from the negative to the positive. I loved you through it all and I miss you.

Love,

Bennie

CHAPTER 4

—Reverend Dr. Alyn E. Waller
"His wisdom goes unmatched as I have referred to many
of his "life lessons" throughout my personal and professional career."

Background/Family

My name is Reverend Dr. Alyn E. Waller, I am 56 years old and live in Pennsylvania. I am originally from Shaker Heights, which is a city outside of Cleveland, Ohio. Shaker Heights was more than just where I was from, it was a place I absolutely loved. It was a trailblazing community, which ensured healthy race relations were the cornerstone of the community's identity. In 1968, our historic city, elected the first African American man as mayor. This moment in time was historic for a number of reasons but what stood out to me the most was the fact that my father served on this historic campaign.

What is unique about where I grew up is that the experience was the great American experience of integration. Shaker Heights is one of the oldest integrated suburbs in the country. Within the city plan of Shaker Heights, no child crosses a major street to walk to their elementary school. There were nine elementary schools that fed into two junior high schools and then one high school. My mother worked for Shaker Heights Housing Authority, where communities were intentionally integrated.

That meant, if you were a black family looking to move into the area, you toured a white neighborhood. It was a very intentional great American experiment, solidifying my beliefs about America and the future: we were meant to be one big community. If you saw the mini-series, *Little Fires Everywhere*, it was all about Shaker Heights.

My Birth

I was born in April of 1964. My mother was from Mount Hope, West Virginia and my father was from Hurt, Virginia. Everyone says I look like my mother, because we both have light features, but as I have gotten older I have seen more of my father's physical traits appear. I still do believe I look more like my mother and my brothers have more of a resemblance to my father but there are many other areas of my life that I totally attribute to my father's influence.

My Hero

The father-son experiences I shared with my father were much different than the experiences each of my brothers shared with our father. My brothers grew up in Pittsburg, at a time when my father was younger and a member of a small church. By the time I was born, my father was 43 years old and in the prime season of his life. Like most men, my father was finally beginning to have some order and clarity in the middle of his life. As I was growing up, it seemed my father found his stride, encouraging me to see him as my hero, but as my brother's got older, they began to show resistance to my father and the church. One of my brothers chose to become a United Methodist pastor and the other brother became Muslim, until recently when he converted back to Christianity.

My father found his stride as I grew but again, the experiences my brothers had with him were very different than what I experienced with him during this stage of his life. My father *gave* me the best of everything.

I would get the best of the best sporting equipment but my father never became too deeply involved. Though I received the best sports equipment, my father actually took my brothers out to the field and played sports *with* them. Our experiences with our father may have been different, but my father was still my hero!

Racism in Ministry

My father was born and grew up in Virginia at a time when racism was significant. He did not graduate from high school until he was 21 years old because there was no colored school for him to attend. My father also experienced racism while in ministry, and the wounds of those events, as a boy, I can still remember.

My school was in Shaker Heights and my father's church was in Central Cleveland. I remember being told I was not "really black" because I was from Shaker Heights. I still carry scars from those experiences, but now, I am unphased by what other people think.

Accepting the Call

My father and I had a good relationship. He was still a man born in 1920, so the gratuitous, "I love you" was rare. Most of what I learned from my father was axiomatic. He always did what he said and did not waiver. He modeled traditional family values. For him, being a man meant being a protector and provider, but not necessarily emotionally present. My father and I became more open with each other after I began preaching. I believe one of my father's proudest moments was when I accepted my call to ministry. Before his passing, we had three beautiful years together where I had the opportunity to preach to him. I learned more from him about being a man and a preacher in those last few years than I learned throughout my entire life. My father died of cancer, which most people did not know because my father was quiet about his illness.

My father was a great revivalist. Back in the days when revivals were five nights, I remember going and listening to my father preach so eloquently. The first time he allowed me to preach he did not let anyone else know. My father was what you would call a wordsmith. He was a wordsmith from Virginia Union. The second night of the revival, my father said, "Tonight, you shall hear me through my loins." That was when he put me up to preach. This was where I began to gain popularity. I became known in Pennsylvania because this happened at the East End Revival in Pittsburgh. The Lord truly blessed me because had I failed that night; I would have gotten us both in trouble. This would be the beginning of many revivals to come.

After preaching on the road, my father and I would go back to our hotel and talk through the events of the day. My father taught me how to read in the house and prepare five nights of preaching. He was a great mentor and taught me life lessons in those moments that I would have otherwise missed. I would never leave a conversation with my father without learning. I remember in 1990, my father gave me the book, *When AIDS Comes to Church*, by William E. Amos Jr. He said, "Alyn, this will not be my ministry, but you will have to deal with this". When he bought the book for me, he said, "you be prepared because this is getting ready to hit our community in a major way." My father was right, and our community suffered in a way I could never have imagined. My father ensured the moments he mentored me and endowed me with wisdom were always purposeful.

Cultural Influences

I am a church kid! I grew up in the church and loved every minute of my experience. My father was a preacher at Shiloh Baptist Church, the oldest African American Black Baptist Church in Cleveland, Ohio. As a child I attended three services every Sunday. I would hang out at my father's church then go next door to the House of Wills. I remember we would have morning service, then we would go over to the House of Wills and play with dead people. We would pretend to have funerals and I always played the preacher. My cousins and I would play church, and we enjoyed it. As you can see church was my life even during times of play.

I enjoyed when my father had guests come preach. Our family would take care of our guests in the church parsonage, a nice house big enough to accommodate the pastors with guest rooms and amenities. I looked forward to the days when the preachers would come stay with us. I would be excited about meeting my father's friends. Some of those friends were Pastor Joseph Harrison Jackson, the longest serving President of the National Baptist Convention, and Samuel DeWitt Proctor, minister, educator, humanitarian and mentor to Dr. Martin Luther King, Jr. My father also went to school with Dr. Wyatt Tee Walker, who was Dr. King's Chief of Staff, as well as civil rights icon, Jesse Jackson, who would often visit. I grew up with some of history's most influential people. My father was prominent in the Civil Rights era. I often show people the picture taken of me as a child, sitting on the lap of Martin Luther King, Jr. He and my father were friends. I remember, in September 1968, when Martin Luther King, Jr. preached my father's fourth pastoral anniversary and I got to sit on his lap on the pulpit. I grew up in and around what is known today as Black history. It was a blessing.

Musicians

My mother and all of my siblings are musicians. My sister is an opera singer living in Weimar, Germany. My sister sounds like Leontyne Price; my oldest brother sings like Sam Cook; my second oldest brother Alexander's style is similar to James Brown. The common thread within our family was music. We all enjoyed it in our own way, and it brought our family together. I personally enjoyed church music. I played the piano and the organ. I also played the trumpet, but it was not needed in church, so I put my efforts into learning to play the piano. I recently began playing the trumpet again. In fact, I am playing my trumpet now because I am doing my midlife negotiation. I am also taking a jazz voice and jazz improvisation class now at Berklee. My goal is to try to learn to sing without the Baptist "hoop." Jazz has always been difficult for me. I often hear and feel the jazz in my head and body but struggle to get it out. Playing the trumpet helps.

Musical Genres

I am learning jazz now because I am enjoying the process of absorbing different genres of music. I am not about to die, but I am retiring in nine years. The pandemic has given me time to think about some of the hobbies I neglected as I drove full steam into ministry and pastoring. I am not sorry for the path I chose but I feel now is a suitable time in my life to reignite some of my former interests.

Church and Politics - "My church is my life"

My church is my life. This is not to say I tout myself as being "super saved". Like most of us, I have wrestled my own demons, but my cultural influences, including the church and politics, have guided many of my decisions. My father was on the campaign for Carl Stokes, the first Black mayor of Cleveland, Ohio, was a contemporary of Leon Sullivan and was instrumental in bringing OIC to Cleveland. These individuals were profound influences on my life and inform how I understand pastors.

My father and I are similar in many ways regarding pastoring but where we differ is when it comes to politics. I truly believe I should be knee deep in voting rights because that is what we should do as leaders, but I also believe there is a line that has to be established. Some of it is because I remember those days in my father's church. Those days were hard, and I have some wounds from those days. I fundamentally understand why he did it, and why pastors of that era did it the way they did; however, that's exactly why I don't do it that way. I don't believe that I should run for anything! I do not let politicians in my pulpit. I did not like it and when my father did it, something felt bad to me about these white men walking in the church, being acknowledged, and then quickly leaving. I do think being politically involved is important but again, I believe there is a line that has to be drawn. My father was involved, and I try to do the same because that is what I saw growing up.

Family Ties

My father and mother met and were married in 1961 and in 1963, he was called to pastor Shiloh Baptist Church. I was born a year later. Shiloh Baptist Church changed the trajectory of his career as a pastor. He was now on "front street" with his ministry. My father became extraordinarily popular. I remember Morehouse College's President, Benjamin Elijah Mays came to our house when my father ran for mayor of Cleveland, Ohio. He said to my father, "You are already the pastor of a major Black church. Why do you want to step down to become mayor"? What he was trying to convey to my father was, if done right, the most influential person in the city could be a Black preacher. These words resonated with my father and he withdrew from the race and put all his efforts into his family and the church. Benjamin Elijah Mays' words of wisdom have always stayed with me.

Fatherly Lessons

My father was a man's man, he taught me to hunt and fish. I am a second amendment type of guy and so was my father. I own many guns. Each Thanksgiving, I hunt and bring something to Thanksgiving dinner. This has become a tradition in my family.

My father taught me that fundamentally, a man takes care of his family. You work hard, so you can play hard. You take care of business, and then, do what you want to do, in that order. I have always believed in taking care of my family, working hard, and making good money to support my family. When my responsibilities are complete, I then take time to enjoy myself.

Fundamentally, I am a conservative Christian, so I believe the definition of manhood includes protection and provision. For me, it is a badge of honor that my wife does not have to work. My father would say, "never let your wife's money have to pay bills." He did not mean that she should not work, but rather my paycheck should take care of my family. And, if my paycheck does not cover the expenses of my family, then I needed to go out and earn more money to support my family.

My father died 1994, right after he installed me. It was such an honor to have him there in celebration with us and my church family. His wisdom goes unmatched, as I have referred to many of his "life lessons" throughout my personal and professional career. He is missed as a giant in the theological world and even more as my father and mentor. His impact and legacy will continue to live on through my family and ministry.

Dear Dad

Dear Dad,

I think I get it now! Thank you for providing me with the foundation to become the man I am today. I cannot imagine how it was for you being a young preacher, alone with your boys after your wife's passing. I am unsure of how you felt after I was born since your professional career was beginning to take off at lightning speed. It is hard to imagine being my age right now having to raise a young child, but that is what you did with me and I thank you.

Thank you for taking time to show and prepare me for what I should strive to become in my own life. Thank you for also recognizing your limitations. I thank you for not letting your limitations constrain your ability to succeed. Thank you for taking care of me and mom and helping me understand how to do this "man" thing. Thank you for helping me be a do-er. I am not sure I know how to be a be-er. For example, I never really learned how to make friends. I am unsure how to fit in with people, as I am not gregarious like you had been. I feel as though people do not enjoy my company and to be honest, I am unsure of what to do or say when I am with a group. I wish you would have shown me how to be more social. I wish you would have shared a bit more with me before the preaching stuff. But, more than anything, I am grateful that I had the honor to be your son.

Love,

Alyn

CHAPTER 5

—Bishop David G. Evans
"Too many nights, my father would come home drunk
and fight with my mother."

At this writing, I am 69 years old. My perception of myself has altered my perspective of the future and most certainly causes a laser-like focus of the past. Wisdom teaches us that time is not wasted if a lesson is learned. As a Philadelphia born, African American man, it was not until recent years I realized an assumed likeness with other black men was a product of an incorrect perception. Many black men, especially those participating in this book, had to "meet" their fathers. I knew my dad, but he was a strange anomaly. A mixture of work ethic, insecurity, strength, visible beauty, and substance affected, melded into the oppression and the impact of race in his lifetime. Born in Camden, NJ, he was an inner-city man striving to better himself, expected to adopt the customary responsibilities of marriage, career and prosperity in an environment designed to defeat him. His move to Philadelphia for work was pivotal for where I would be born. A bridge built in the memory of Benjamin Franklin, a 13-minute ride from Camden to Philadelphia, decided the location difference which began my journey.

I was born in Philadelphia but moved to Chester, PA after my parents' divorce. We moved from black upper middle class to the Fairground Projects in Chester, PA; one of the most challenging places to live in the nation at present. It had a tremendous impact on my life. I was raised by a single mom pursuing her college degree during the day, working, and studying at night. My grandparents, who lived in the same project housing, helped in consistently heroic ways. Grandad, the epitome of strength, faith, fairness, courage, and balance became "dad". What my father lacked, my grandfather possessed in excess.

I was born in the 1950s, a unique time to be African American. Racial tension was everywhere but the projects, at that time, were slightly integrated. Outside of the projects was where my family and I experienced racial tension and oppression. This became the backdrop of my life. As a result, when it comes to matters of race, fairness, and equality, I find myself extremely sensitive.

My extended family is from the South, i.e., Savannah, Georgia, Jacksonville, Florida, and, Norfolk, Virginia. My dad, from Camden, NJ and my mom from Florida, crossed paths. My grandfather, Albert Prince, was a militant. Experience can shape perspective and reactions. He experienced the full civil rights pendulum swing. One night in Savannah, a mob of Ku Klux Klan hooded men assembled on the front lawn of my grandparents' home. Crosses were burning and men were shouting threats while standing on my grandparent's perfectly manicured front lawn. Initially, my grandfather, rifle in hand, confronted them alone. Within minutes, my grandmother was by his side. He told her to go inside. She said, "I'll die out here with you." They did not believe they would survive the night.

My grandfather told the angry mob that at least three of the Klansmen would die with them. The KKK backed off and my grandparents chose to relocate soon after. They had been one of the first black families in Savannah to own their property. My grandfather was intelligent. You see, when trains ran by coal, my grandfather was the one who coaled the train. The updated version of the Champion still runs from Jacksonville, FL to Philadelphia, PA. My grandfather negotiated a deal with his boss to coal the train alone from Jacksonville to Philadelphia and back for one and a half times the salary. He did this for years. His work ethic provided my grandparents, aunts, and uncles with a living most blacks did not have at the time. They were able to move from Savannah to Jacksonville and later north to Chester, PA. They settled in the Fairground Projects in Chester, PA. My grandfather became the night security guard at a major bank and eventually served as Chairman of the Deacon Board at Bethany Baptist Church in Chester, PA. I grew up in this church, building my faith and positively shaping my life after we left my father.

Who am I?

Background/Family

My younger brother was an "arm" baby, needing constant attention. I was always a responsible child. At three or four years old, my mother never worried about me being alone or misbehaving in someone else's care. In her words, "He had always been a man." In my childhood pictures, I wore a sports jacket, ironed shirt, and always had one hand in my pocket. When I see the pictures, I understand my mother's words. Most of those pictures are absent of my father. Experience can force calm maturity upon you. There are events and situations early in life you never forget that shape perception and perspective. For me, it was when my parents were officially divorced.

We were living in the projects. Mom was talking to my father upstairs. I was listening to the conversation at the bottom of the stairs in the dark. I understood from Mom's responses my father was going to marry his girlfriend because she was pregnant. I was confused and could not understand why my father was worrying about someone else's child when he was doing nothing for us.

The transition from our home in West Philadelphia to Chester was drastic. In the 1950's and 1960's, the area around us was a showplace. The apartment where we lived encompassed an entire level of a house – two/three bedrooms, dining room, and kitchen. The neighborhood was a melting pot of sorts – Jewish, Polish, African American, Asian. Everyone knew each other. My dad earned $30/hour, decent money. He taught himself how to set type (including color) and did this for the Daily News, the Bulletin and Inquirer. For a black man in the 50s and 60s, that was a ton of money. We had the best of everything. Then you juxtapose that to the Fairground Projects, government projects, government food, powdered milk, and eggs and government cheese. My mother had an internal drive and motivation no person could slow. As a family, we have always been proud of our heritage, knowing our relatives had been slaves, were emancipated, and then became successful.

Influences

I do not believe my father positively influenced my foundational upbringing. He worked but was an alcoholic and he fought my mother. These experiences were negative, but mom's example positively affected my work ethic, taught me how to care for myself, my family and those in my community. My mother never commented on our physical appearance or intelligence. She simply reminded us to be aware of our presence and try our best to be successful. Mom taught us how to be honest and respectable men during a time when the world had nothing but hostility toward Black men.

My dad was a non-entity but I was lucky to have a strong extended family. I had my grandparents and aunts, three of which married progressive, educated Black men. Higher education surrounded me. Entrepreneurial and corporate spirits were instilled in us. Most of the family was athletic. Being one-dimensional was unacceptable. We aimed to excel in everything. We never heard, "Do well in sports, and you do not have to go to school." In our home, if you did poorly in school, sports privileges were revoked. Discipline was strong in our home and children did not question their elders.

Looking back, it was my mother's side of the family that really inspired me. They set the standard for me. My life trajectory could have been remarkably different had I followed in the steps of other people. I might have emulated my father, which, to me, is highly offensive. I made a promise to myself to always protect my mother, doing everything in my power to prevent her from ever crying tears of pain or shame. I kept my word until the day my mother passed. I know I made her proud.

We were a renaissance family, education, vocation, arts and, sports-focused – all at the same time. It was common for us to get together at family dinners and discuss everything from politics, to the most influential musician of the moment. It did not hurt having young Martin Luther King Jr., Rev. Ralph D. Abernathy and other civil rights heroes eating in our kitchen twice a month. My grandfather was Chairman of the Deacon Board at Bethany Baptist Church in Chester, PA, one of the leading African American Churches in the region. At that time, Crozier Theological Seminary was also located in Chester.

Bethany was a mandatory stop for all Crozier Seminary students at least twice a month. Each time Martin Luther King, Jr., William Augustus Jones, Jr., Samuel D. Proctor came to Bethany, my grandfather brought them home for dinner. He openly welcomed that type of company. He was pro-black, wanting the best for all members of the community, both locally and globally. I remember my grandfather watching Marquette in the NCAA basketball championship. He was so passionate about the game, knowing that an all-black basketball team was a historical change in the sports landscape. He always provided us with a pro-African American, pro-Black, proud black, educated environment.

Growing up I learned a lot about my dad. I learned his priorities: he chose alcohol over food for us and women were higher on his list of priorities than clothes for his children. He was a drunk and not ashamed to be non-functional. I learned quickly what not to do as a man. Surprisingly, my father was a functional alcoholic. He would go to work every day, get drunk at work during a break, and sober up by the time he had to return to work. He would drink straight through the weekend, until Sunday afternoon, when, like clockwork, he would stop and get ready for work again. My father's influence was incredibly negative, but I learned from him how to NOT treat others and how to not ignore my responsibilities. I try not to paint too negative a picture of my father. To this day, I believe my father was an alcoholic, because he was trying to anesthetize his frustration. What African American man independently teaches himself calculus, algebra, architecture, and becomes a black belt in karate? His interests were science, math, and history. Yet, with all that intelligence, he found himself at a glass ceiling, frustrated with not being able to get ahead, to the level he thought he should be able to obtain.

As I have gotten older, my understanding for my father's frustration has increased and my desire for closure has decreased. Closure is important but overrated because there are some people, feelings, challenges, or events one can intellectually accept, while others that are emotionally unacceptable, because they never should have happened. I believe everyone should have the opportunity for a closure conversation with the person who caused emotional harm. Hopefully, this would allow the hurt individual to get answers to the questions they were longing to ask. Personally, I would have wanted this moment of clarity, to understand why my father abandoned us, but even if I had all the answers, I still do not believe full closure would have been possible.

Growing up I saw many family members saved from a life of reckless danger. We had many cultural and spiritual influences; my uncle was a self-taught pianist and entertainer. We grew up attending performances. My aunts would listen to jazz. I still have old Miles Davis' albums. My own collection of R&B goes back to the Ohio Players, Stevie Wonder, Sly and the Family Stone, who sparked a music revolution, also including the Beatles and the Rolling Stones. We experienced an eclectic mix, a melting pot of cultural influence, but always centered around pro-blackness and a powerful sense of spirituality. If you were not in tune with God, your education, and the importance of being an upstanding human being, you were not welcome in my family. Amid poverty, we remained positive and focused on these principles.

Challenges

I think my biggest challenge has been isolation. My perspective is somewhat different from others. It has not been one that has garnered many close friends. However, it has produced a work that most well-informed people, especially in the African American community, acknowledge as being successful. Acceptance by my peers has been my biggest challenge. I realize my preaching and pastoring is different. I must also admit, the internal voice of my father's temptation was a seasonal challenge felt but never responded to in my youth.

Struggles

The separation of my parents was the absolute best decision for my family. Too many nights, my father would come home drunk and fight with my mother. A tomboy of sorts, my mother could hold her own. I felt I was meant to be her protector but, more importantly, she should never have to defend herself.

One morning, I hit my breaking point. I was only five years old, but I clearly remember my father stumbling through the door as I was leaving for school and immediately going after my mother. I walked to the front door and propped it open with my book bag. I had planned my escape. I walked back to the kitchen and grabbed a roasting fork with six-inch prongs. I found my dad and stabbed him in the hand, leaving the fork jammed into his hand. I left him there, bleeding and ran out the open door, grabbing my bag along the way.

I was nervous to come home from school as I was unsure of what to expect. My father approached me and said, "You did not like what I did to your mom." I angrily responded, "No, and if you ever do it again, I am going to kill you." My father knew I was serious and never laid a hand on my mother again.

Soon after, my mother divorced my father. She did not want him to be our role model. She struggled, working two and three jobs, while also going to college. A strong work ethic was etched into my very being. My mother not only attended but excelled in school. I watched as she accomplished two advanced degrees. She did all of this as a single woman, raising two boys. My mother overcame her struggles. She was my hero. We were poor and never knew it. We wore secondhand clothes, which were always in excellent condition. We never went hungry. We lived in the projects but we had a manicured lawn always lined with rose bushes. We were able to leave our doors open in the summer, because we were not in danger of unwelcome company. No one locked their houses in the summer because there was no air conditioning. We would all sleep in the backyard. But when the influence of drugs became prevalent, the culture changed, and this feeling of freedom disappeared.

Impact of My Father Not Being There

My mother and grandparents did everything they could to compensate for the absence of my father. I remember feeling a sadness when I saw other boys with their fathers. But I knew my family was doing everything in their power to give my brother and me a successful future. I learned to adapt quickly. I do not think something was wrong with my father, but I do think something was missing. In hindsight, it is ridiculous and risky to expect someone, with his level of dysfunction, to change and do right by others.

After my parents separated, I quickly became the "man" of the house. I did most of the housework so my mother would come home to a clean house. I made sure my brother did his homework and ate the food my mother had prepared. My responsibilities increased and I welcomed the challenge. I have always taken care of people. My brother's job was to follow my mother's directions. My mother's job was to provide security for all of us. We all did our jobs to the best of our abilities. The support we had was phenomenal.

When I was 13 years old, my brother and I went to visit my father. He did not answer the door. A neighbor told us he had moved down south.

No warning.

No good-bye.

Nothing.

We never saw my father again. Years later, we heard he died from cirrhosis of the liver. My mother showed no reaction when she heard of my father's death. For me, it was as if the weight of the world finally lifted off my shoulders. He was not the father he should have been to us.

I never felt that I needed counseling to work through my emotions about my father. He had not been around. To me, that was straightforward and did not deserve more discussion. After he left, he tried to make a few appearances. I remember the night of my prom, I arrived home late, and he called to see if I had gotten home safely. He began to lecture me about time, but I would have no part of the conversation. I told him he did not have the right to speak with me about this issue and if necessary, I would discuss it with my mother. I felt strongly that when he chose to abandon us, he also elected to give up the right to discuss these types of situations with me. My grandfather did everything he could to make sure I did not miss my father. My grandfather was an unusual African American man, ethical, well-spoken, physically strong and imposing, yet gentle, someone who could have gone further, had opportunities been presented.

We lived as structured and consistent a life as possible. Learning how to care for others helped me heal my own wounds. I felt that being a father-like figure to others helped ease my feelings of abandonment.

During my sophomore year in high school, I started testing my boundaries at home. I started talking back to my mom, acting like a typical rowdy teenager. Many of the local gangs tried to recruit me. I remember being at a party, talking to the sister of a gang member. He did not like us talking and he pushed me. I hit him so hard in his chest that he fell to the ground. Several weeks after the party, a gang member came to the house. He gave me the choice to either join the gang or fight every member, one after another. I fought all nine and did not join the gang. Fear of Mom and fighting skills helped me in high school.

My mom did not like the attitude I was starting to present. She sent me to boarding school – the Church Farm School in Exton, PA. We wore blazers, ties, white shirts, slacks, and dress shoes to class each day. Had I not gone to the Church Farm School, I probably would not be where I am today. Structure is a key to success. Every hour of the day was structured.

College

The academic stress of the Church Farm School was intense, with report cards sent home every six weeks. I had to take part in three sports a year and became conference champion in hurdles and wrestling. I participated in many activities and events. Moving onto college, I briefly sought to join a fraternity. During a hazing ritual, some of us recruits embarrassed members of the fraternity. As punishment, they decided they were going to paddle us. At the time, Lincoln University was notorious for brutal, sometimes fatal pledging rituals. Once, a brother was blind folded, walked out on the highway and was hit by a car. That changed everything. I withdrew from pledging. I worked full time and went to school full time for three years, keeping a 3.0 GPA, with a double major. My college days were good. During the first year of college, I became a father and immediately realized I had to take care of my child. I worked full time, while in school. I moved off campus near Chester, PA. Unlike my father, I did what I had to do to support the obligations I had created for myself.

Social Interests

We grew up on film noir, Hitchcock, Orson Wells, as well as Earl Flynn, Burt Lancaster, and cowboy movies. My nickname was Tex because I liked cowboys. As kids, we also had a fascination with comic books. I had an extraordinary collection. It would be worth a sizeable amount of money today. I owned two of everything - Batman, Superman, Fantastic Four, Hulk, you name it, I had it. I had one to read, one to keep. When my brother heard I was planning to come home from my first year of college, he wanted to do something special for me. He made a collage from the covers of the comic books. I know his heart was in the right place, but he destroyed my comic books. My mother had to calm me because I wanted to kill him! I had a phenomenal collection, lost through a childish desire to make something pretty. I still like mysteries and cowboy movies. I think my favorite cowboy movie is "Shane with Allen Lad." One of the more recent is "True Grit" and my all-time favorite is "The Magnificent Seven." Movies spoke to me more than television. Unlike my friends, I never enjoyed "The Fresh Prince of Bel Air" or "The Cosby Show." If I had to choose a television genre, I suppose I would choose comedy; however, those shows were not my favorite.

Career

After I graduated, I began to work a job in the banking industry as a financial analyst. I found a meteoric career in banking. My colleagues and I would attend lenders meetings, where only a handful of Black lenders were at the AVP, VP level. I was the number one producer at my bank. As a VP, I was the head of the division, controlling loans from all branches for half of the state. My predecessor at one of the banks was a Caucasian gentleman, who had failed in the position. I brought structure to the position and trained branch managers to responsibly lend money.

I experienced racism in the banking industry. The most profound incident was when an executive board member asked, "How does it feel to be the missing link between apes and men?" I looked around the room, hoping my boss would come to my aid. When no one spoke, I sat back in my chair and outlined the differences between my human characteristics and those of an ape. While it was never directly spoken, my comparison turned the tables, making the others seem more like apes than anyone else. I knew what I was doing and what I was saying. I chose my words carefully, knowing full well there was a strong possibility I would lose my job. I accepted this, as I knew jobs would come and go but my self-worth was forever. Surprisingly, I was not fired but the entire exchange made me rethink my position.

After some time had passed, I asked for a raise. The company offered me 3%, saying that was the best they could do. I knew the reason was the color of my skin, not my talent and expertise in the field. I was the highest producer in the region with a fee income of about fifty million dollars. I went back to my office and reviewed my portfolio to see which business would take the lowest amount of capital input and give me the highest yield. It was building maintenance. A customer I knew, with no high school education was making a million dollars a year and had been for the last 25 years. We spoke privately and I decided to subcontract with him, leaving my job and overt racism behind. When our contract expired, I partnered with two major bakeries in Philadelphia – Nabisco and Tastykake. In addition, I began contracting with chains of dialysis centers and servicing more than 400 homes for the blind. My businesses were expanding. My mother, who had an outstanding catering service, introduced me to entrepreneurship. I had worked with her as a boy, setting up, serving, and cleaning. As a youngster, I saw how to run a business independently and followed in my mother's footsteps. While in business, my interest in politics developed.

Life Lessons – Passed to My Children

I think I have taught my children some important lessons and I try to prepare them for life after my passing. I remind them of the difference between right and wrong, to love and serve God, do the right thing, think of others, work hard, smart and get an education.

Whether my children emulate my beliefs is up to them. If nothing else, they will know I tried to teach them *how* to think instead of *what* to think. Because of our stress levels, I believe African American parents tend to tell children what, not how, to think. Mistakes often pass from one generation to the next. The legacy of a parent's voice should be one a child refers to for strength and guidance during challenging times.

Greatest Accomplishment

I believe I have managed to be a ground breaker, and landscape changer everywhere I have gone. I have excelled in all my careers, including finding my perfect job, my calling, which is pastoring God's people. I think that sense of accomplishment has afforded me the greatest gift, which is to positively affect the lives of others. For the last 30 years, God has helped and guided me as I have helped and guided others.

Adjectives

Four adjectives to describe my father are:

Intelligent – He was able to teach himself skills that people have had to go to college to learn. He could build anything. He could teach himself anything – scientific theories, calculus, algebra, trigonometry, phenomenal artist, taught himself drafting. He was an unbelievable swimmer. He was a conversationalist but was not strong enough to resist the peer pressure of the place where he worked.

Frustrated – He was frustrated because of the ceiling that existed for African American men back in his day. I know he felt forced to perform at levels lower than his ability.

Addictive – Anesthetizing his frustration and the inability to progress like he thought he should, because of his intelligence and gifts.

Unavailable – there was nothing wrong with him, something was just missing.

Letter to Dad

Dear Dad,

The older I have gotten, the more I have been able to understand why you led the life you did. From your poor choices, I learned to honor, cherish, and appreciate my mother. I thank you for that.

Dave

CHAPTER 6

—Yvesmark Chery
"His strictness brought my siblings and I together,
because we all shared this bond."

Background/Family

My father's religious background influenced the origin of my name. My father combined the St. Yves from his Catholic upbringing and Evangelist Mark from his Baptist background and my name was not only created but it had meaning. My parents are from Haiti and immigrated to the United States during the 1980s. I was born August 28, 1996, in Brooklyn, New York but raised in Philadelphia, Pennsylvania and currently live in the Northeast section of the city.

I am the second youngest of six siblings, I have three older sisters, one older brother and one younger sister. I was raised by my parents and elder siblings. In our household, there was one thing for sure, our parents were extraordinarily strict. My eldest sister always tried challenging our strict parents. For example, my parents were "clear" about women only wearing dresses and skirts and my eldest sister led a humble revolt. Years later, her efforts paid off because now my youngest sister wears pants freely. On a scale of one to ten, I rate my upbringing a ten. While my parents were my foundation, my siblings have always been my support system. They were open to sharing their experiences with me, more than my parents. My parent's Haitian culture strongly influenced all of us. Without question, we had a resound reverence for respecting our parents, made spirituality a priority, and continually aimed to live a life of happiness.

I grew up in a two-parent household but that was not the story of my father. My father grew up without his father in his life. He never spoke about how growing up without his father affected him and though I always wondered, I never felt there was an appropriate time to ask. However, later in life, he reconciled with his father. When my father received the call that his father was extremely ill in the hospital, he rushed to his bedside, and was blessed enough to finally have a heartfelt conversation with him. It seemed like my father forgave my grandfather for not being there, and my father and grandfather were now at peace. In 2017, my grandfather passed. I believe forgiveness plays a huge part in moving on with life.

In Haiti, my mother and father's family knew each other well and my parents knew of each other. When my father saw my mother for the first time, he was enamored by her beauty. My father made attempts to speak to her, but a relationship would not be possible as my mother was preparing to move to the United States. She moved soon after and my father could do nothing but follow her. My father moved to the United States, taking a risk as he had never even spoken to my mother! It was only after my father settled in the United States that they began their relationship... and as they say, the rest is history.

Parental Influence/Upbringing

My older siblings helped enforce my parents' teachings even though they may have disagreed with them. Through their life experiences, I learned how to appropriately carry myself, regardless of the situation. My parents had a strong influence on who I am today. My grandfather did not raise my father. My father did not have this male role model growing up and when my siblings and I were growing up, he was extremely strict which I believe was in direct correlation to my grandfather's absence. However, my mother, raised by both of her parents, was the more relaxed of the two. She would let us experience life firsthand, while standing guard from a distance.

My father was more lenient with me than my siblings, probably because I was obedient and followed directions. Because of my father's Haitian upbringing, there were behaviors he did not find acceptable. For example, we were forbidden to sleep over anyone's house – friends or family. Secular music was not permitted. We were only allowed to listen to gospel music. There were times (even now) I would be around someone playing music and I do not recognize the artist or band, because of lack of exposure. Now that I am older, I understand why my father held so many of the beliefs he did, however I wish he had been more lenient when it came to certain American behaviors. My father's strict upbringing made my siblings and I better people, and closer to God. His strictness brought my siblings and I together because we all shared this bond. Now that we are adults, our father is more tolerant and accepting of our choices.

My father's stringency was a challenge for my siblings and me, because everything we saw outside of the home was in opposition of my parents' traditional Haitian upbringing. We experienced a battle between our cultural upbringing and the "norms" of the American culture surrounding us. My sister wanted to wear jeans but my parents only allowed skirts. My parents would use religion as the background for why we could not take part in certain activities or behaviors, such as wearing earrings or getting a tattoo. The strictness was a considerable challenge as we grew older. We wanted our freedom. Now that I am older, I thank my father for what we considered a restrictive upbringing. I believe it provided discipline and a sense of pride in who I represent as a Black man in America.

My role models were my older brother Daniel and my pastor, Dr. Allen E. Waller. My brother was the class clown. Everyone thought he was funny. I would look at him and say, "I want that too!" I have always looked up to him. Not only was he funny, but he had wisdom and gave sound advice. He was always encouraging to people. I have always looked to him as a leader amongst his peers. Many people say he is a good man! Currently, he is my modeling stylist. I too, aspire to be the one that encourages other people.

My other role model is my pastor, Dr. Allen E. Waller. He has the amazing gift of making scripture accessible, spiritually feeding my soul. I admire him greatly. He is an amazing human. It is easy to spot the wrong in the world. I want to be able to emulate his light – for my family, friends, anyone who needs hope, help and support in their relationship with God. I want to be that hope for someone, encouraging their belief that a better future is possible.

Physical Appearance/Characteristics

I look more like my mother. I get certain features, such as the fullness of my lips from my mother. My ears come from my father. I have Vitiligo, which is an auto immune condition that causes a loss of pigmentation. The first time I realized I had Vitiligo, I was four or five years old. I told my parents I had something on my face. It started as a small speck. I thought it was dirt; and I tried to wash it off. My parents are Certified Nursing Assistants, and, in addition, my dad is an herbalist. They did not know what Vitiligo was at first. After we tried to wash it off, we went to the doctor and then a dermatologist who diagnosed my skin condition as Vitiligo. I believe my parents felt bad, because they did not want me to experience the physical changes that were happening. Especially since they knew children could be cruel.

There were topical medications that worked initially but as a child, it was not my priority to take/apply the medication. Even if it went away a little bit, the results were temporary, and it always came back. My dad was always searching for different herbs and concoctions to cure my condition. Growing up in Philadelphia, people were cruel. I was teased, called a tiger, a zebra. When I was 13 years old, I remember being outside, and a group of teenagers were walking past me. One of them exclaimed, "What the Fuck?!" They all started laughing which made me feel hurt, ashamed, and angry. I would get weird stares. Even today, there are occasions when I am paying a bill at a store and the cashier does not want to touch my hand. I used to allow it to affect my mood but today I realize that people are just ignorant to the lack of knowledge. Currently, because of my modeling and being an advocate for Vitiligo, it is more widely understood and accepted.

I refer to my Vitiligo as my skin condition. I believe *disease* has negative connotations. People often believe it to be contagious, which is very much not the case. Many believed Michael Jackson had Vitiligo. Growing up, I did not connect to his story, as there was always speculation about its legitimacy. Now, I believe there are similarities; I can relate to him, because I know he had my skin condition, and probably had some similar experiences. I have a few friends with the same skin condition. There was a time I wanted my Vitiligo off my face. I never thought about bleaching my skin, but I did want the Vitiligo off my face. I thought if it was off my face, I could make more friends. My rationale was that I was already making friends with Vitiligo on my face, imagine if it was off my face? Now I realize that people love and accept differences and I love that. Over time, I have grown to love my skin condition. Now, I make sure to express that I love my skin. I no longer search for creams or medications. I have come to accept the skin God chose for me.

My upbringing gave me the strength and fortitude to handle all that has come my way. I constantly reflect on my father's influence in my life. His forceful intentions were for our well-being. I feel blessed to have had his strong, positive influence in my life. I am also blessed that he instilled such strong religious beliefs in us because growing up with a skin condition, sometimes my faith was all I had to rely on and it made it easier.

Father's teachings

My father used his own experiences to teach my siblings and me how to approach and manage life. He always stressed that education was the key to success. Additionally, he frequently discussed his belief in God and how He was the head of our lives. My father taught us so much about education, religion, and maturity. Additionally, he taught us about finances. He used his experiences as examples of what to pursue and what to avoid. The lessons my father taught me helped shape the man I have become. I grew up respecting his leadership, knowing my place as a child, and his as the head of our household. As strong Haitian individuals, my parent's cultural foundation molded my siblings and I.

Relationship with parents

As an adult, my relationship with my parents is different than it was when I was a child. When I was younger, our relationship was parent-child. They raised me in the way that made sense to them. Growing up, I did not have a relationship with them. I earned good grades to please them and to ultimately get what I wanted. I thought if I pleased them, they would not bother me and give me what I wanted when I asked for something. Now that I am older, I have more of a relationship with them. I feel comfortable going to them with certain issues, such as asking for relationship advice.

My relationship with my father – I believe we have overcome a communication barrier. Before, our relationship was strictly a father-son relationship. There was no friend aspect to it. Now, I call my father my friend. I can joke with him. Even the trivial things, like using slang – I can do now. When growing up, responses were always respectful, such as "Yes Sir, Yes Ma'am." Now I can say "Y,erp, What's good?" He is receptive to my joking with him. We can also talk about girls. Even recently, my father asked me "When are you going to settle down?" and I said, "Slow your roll Pops." I enjoy how our relationship has evolved.

Because of his strictness, I did not always like my father. One night during Revival, a night church service, I talked to my father and expressed to him, "I forgive you." He did not understand but for me, this is when the dynamic of our relationship changed. It was a fresh start. I let go of any ill-feelings I had from my strict upbringing. I know that my parents' strong spiritual and religious beliefs guided how they raised us and I know it was for our good.

Religion

My father is Christian. He is Baptist. When he was in Haiti, he was Catholic. I am also Baptist. As a child, I was deep into my relationship with God. I studied the Bible, not because I had to, but because I enjoyed my relationship with God. When I turned 12 years old, I made the conscious decision to give my life to Christ. This was because of the foundation my father instilled in us.

I remember times when I was angry with my father and looking up scripture to support my beliefs. I would Google verses from the Bible, such as, *You have to train up a child in the way he should go, (Proverbs 22:6)*, so I could follow my passion. However, I tried to finesse the system my parents put in place trying to use their teachings to fit my wrong at the time.

Girlfriends

As a result of my religious upbringing, I set boundaries for myself related to romantic relationships that I felt aligned with my spiritual beliefs. When I was growing up, my mindset was deeply religious. I wanted to save myself for marriage. I was not interested in putting myself in a position to cross boundaries that I was not ready for; like having a girlfriend. A lot of people did not *see* my skin, because of my personality. It was not hard to make friends. I did not want a girlfriend because of the religious aspect but I was a flirt for sure!

When I was in college, out of curiosity, coupled with the influence of my friends, I made the choice to lose my virginity. Because of the mindset I was in, I have no regrets. There were other variables that led up to me losing my virginity. I believe everything happens for a reason. It was one of those situations that I now see as *it is what it is*. Live and learn.

For me, I develop relationships by knowing the other person's intentions. It was important for me to know what I wanted and where I was at the time. At times, I would bring girls home, who might be a prospective girlfriend. I knew that because of my parents' mindset, I could not share everything with them. If I brought a girl home, I brought her to meet my siblings.

When I was young, I had to be home by a certain time. When I got to high school, earned good grades (3.9 GPA), and did everything my parents wanted, they let me have my fun. They were strict with my other siblings but because I was obedient, they were less strict with me.

Education

I had to be home by a certain time no matter what. When I got to high school, earned good grades (3.9 GPA), and did everything my parents wanted, they let me have my fun. They were strict with my other siblings but because I was obedient, they were less strict with me. I attended a Philadelphia Public High school. My favorite teacher was my senior high school teacher. He was relatable. We could joke around with him. He was someone you could be real with; he did not "sugar coat" his beliefs and told us the hard truth about life.

For college, I attended the Pennsylvania State University – Main Campus. Leaving my traditional Haitian household for college was an eye-opening experience, as this was the first time in my life that I had complete freedom to make my own decisions. I used this opportunity to explore different ideas, beliefs, and music. However, my parents' teachings always kept me grounded and disciplined. As a result, the transition from high school to college was not difficult. But my excitement for the numerous opportunities that were available led to my grades dropping. This included extra-curricular activities with my college fraternity. Eventually, I realized I had to refocus my priorities and improve my grades if I wanted to be successful after I graduated from college. My dad's strictness helped me get closer to God which, in turn, made me focus on my academics.

Career

I have always focused on my goals. Becoming a model was not my original plan. My degree is in Information Science Technology. When I was in college, my ex-girlfriend was a model. She always commented on my facial features and encouraged me to model. She knew what the agencies and casting directors wanted. While I was still in college, she registered me for a random casting call in New York. When I went, everyone was very encouraging. One person said they wanted my skin condition! I decided to stick with it, and it became a blessing. I am using my undergraduate degree by working for an information technology corporation but modeling is currently my true passion. I have worked on many campaigns, like Ivy Park, Calvin Klein, Adidas, Barney's, Tom Brown, GQ, and Verizon, as well as magazines like Flaunt and Essence. I have only been in the industry for about two years. I also do runway modeling. I did a digital show for this year's fashion week. I am grateful for the experiences. My father was not necessarily thrilled with my choice of modeling after college graduation and wanted me to have "back up" plans in place.

I have several professional paths. I invest in real estate; I work for Apple, and I model. I have goals for each path. For real estate, my goal is to purchase more properties before the end of next year. In terms of Apple, I would like to continue advancing to higher positions with different responsibilities. In terms of modeling, I would like to increase my high fashion campaigns. However, in modeling, there have been times when agencies presented me with requests that made me uncomfortable. One time, during fashion week, I went to the fitting and was asked to wear heels. I informed them that wearing heels did not align with my beliefs. I did not continue working with that company. Having the courage to walk away from job opportunities that challenge my core belief system is important to me. I know that my father's example leads me to being such a strong individual, not compromising my beliefs for a paycheck.

Inspirations

Each day, I find new inspirations and make decisions that will influence my future. For example, I remember traveling home from New York on the train. While en route, I saw a family with four children. While not passing judgement on the family's choice to travel by train, I distinctly remember thinking I would not want my own children to travel this way. Because I did not want this for myself, I found it to be inspiring, as I would have to plan to have the financial means to ensure different transportation for my family.

I want to be there for my children. My father taught me that when children are young, they are not friends with their parents. The responsibility of a parent is to guide the child along the right path, supporting their dreams and passions as they evolve. I believe I will always support my children's interests, but I know I will expect them to put their studies first. I want to be supportive and caring while ensuring that my children know their boundaries. There will come a time for talking about boys/girls. I want to guide my child on their path to success.

The one non-negotiable belief I would pass down from my father is my love for God. I would bring my children to church, so they would understand my interactions with God through prayer. I believe it is important for my children to be exposed to my experiences, both past and present.

Three adjectives to describe my father are:

Funny – Looking back, when he was punishing us, he was funny. It was not funny back then.

Talkative – My father can talk your ear off. There was a time, when we were younger, that we would prefer getting a whipping, as opposed to being talked to about our transgression for hours.

Loving – Although he was strict, I know it was out of love. He made many sacrifices, such as not going to school, because he was taking care of his family.

My Story – I define myself as:

1. Christian

2. Black Male

3. A model with Vitiligo

I do not want my brand to be the Vitiligo model. I want it to be the Christian Black Male *with* Vitiligo.

Letter to Dad

Dear Dad,

First, I want to say thank you. Although things were not always great in my early childhood, I am older now and understand why you made the choices you did. I am very appreciative of you. Just know that all your efforts, demanding work, and sacrifices you made for me and my siblings did not go unnoticed.

I know there are certain goals you want to accomplish now that my siblings and I are older. I want you to live the rest of your days not worrying about your children, financial aspects of life or anything that could disrupt your peace of mind. I want you to worry about yourself, your wife and enjoy the latter years. I know you will not be here with me forever. I am very thankful for everything you have instilled in me. Thank you for the relationship that you helped inspire between my siblings and me. I want you to be happy. I know that you are proud of all of us. I just want you to know that I am ok, we are all ok and to sit back and allow us to show you what we have learned from your guidance.

Your loving son,

Yvesmark

CHAPTER 7

—Bishop Keith W. Reed Sr.
"My dad struggled with the emotional challenges of his past…
He definitely taught me the importance
of being a leader and not a follower."

My name is Keith Reed. To many people, I am Bishop Reed. I was born in North Philadelphia in 1957, during the Vietnam War era. It was the time of the civil rights movement with Dr. Martin Luther King Jr. and the Motown explosion influencing music culture. It was the time of Black Power, filled with racial tension, such as with the Black Panthers and Frank Rizzo as the former mayor of Philadelphia. We lived in two separate project units within the same housing complex. The unit I was born in was a small three-bedroom row home and when I was ten years old, we moved into a corner unit, with four bedrooms, literally in the backyard of our first row home. We were moving up in life.

In addition to racial tension, there were many gang wars. Where I grew up, gangs were everywhere. Fortunately, I was never "drafted" to join a gang. Many of my cousins were members of the local gang so they left my brother and me alone. However, I did participate in some of the devious activities while hanging around with my cousins. Looking back there were times that I know that God was protecting me. One night we all went to engage in a gang turf war. I remember being scared deep in my soul, but I knew not to show it in my face. When the police arrived, we ran.

I now know that was a blessing. If the police officers had not shown up it could have turned into something terrible that could have changed my life forever.

I remember the time when we stole some hospital garments off a freight train. We put them on to disguise ourselves to look like members of the KKK so the police would leave us alone. We would drink, steal, frequent house parties, anything and everything that was not beneficial to our lives. Even though it was risky, I believe these events and decisions were meant to be part of my journey.

My Parents' Influence

My Mother

My mother was the nurturer, she was *there* most of the time. She was also the 'financial wiz' of the family. My father made the money, but my mom handled it. She would dress us up and take us to my father's job to get his paycheck before it made it into his hands. That way there was no chance he would waste it drinking or partying with his friends. That process was never embarrassing for my father. I remember the look on his face when we would walk into his place of work. We would always be very cleanly dressed, and he always looked so proud. His face would boast 'these are my children, and this is my wife'. We would make the rounds as he introduced us to everyone, each co-worker putting 50 cents in our pockets as we passed. My mother taught us 'you can live in the ghetto, but the ghetto does not have to live in you'. Yes, we lived in the projects, but I knew no one else lucky enough to have wall to wall carpeting. My mother bought a real sterling silverware set and taught us how to set the table, not just on Thanksgiving but throughout the year. She made that house a castle for my father and her children.

Yes, we went to the Moreland Center, to get the food they gave to low-income people, but my mother made that a meal fit for a king. They would give us big blocks of cheese and SPAM. When that SPAM came out of the can, it looked disgusting. I have no idea how my mom did it, but she made SPAM soufflé, SPAM sandwiches, SPAM on salad and it always looked so delicious. I did not know we were poor until I moved out of the projects. I never went to bed hungry and I always had clothes and shoes. Looking back now, I am amazed at how powerful my mother was in those formidable years. I had no idea how much she was investing into my own future and the lessons she was teaching all of us. She taught me to see potential in everything. My mom's SPAM showed me that I always have an opportunity to make something great out of something that seems fruitless. It cultivated an attitude of hope and prosperity in my life that still exists today.

My Father

I have been told that I am a *perfect likeness to* my father. It is almost like my mother had nothing to do with it. I truly am my father's son. My father was large in my life, a giant. I thought he could do everything. He modeled the importance of hard work. His leadership skills were innate. He could get a job without even trying! As soon as he received a job, it was only a matter of months until he made it to the top to become a supervisor. At one time, he was working in security and within six months promoted to lieutenant. They gave him the uniform, but they could not give him the pay because the raise was based on how much time he was on the job. He was performing all the responsibilities without receiving the pay because his skills were so sharp. He taught me the importance of being a leader and not a follower.

My dad struggled with the emotional challenges of his past. He was active in World War II and the psychological damage of his experience pushed him to self-medicate with alcohol. There were times my father would go on a drinking binge, not report to work and then lose his job. I would watch him get off a binge, shave his face, get his stuff together and get another job for his family. I would not necessarily call that positive but looking back now, that is the pattern I remember.

One night after my dad had just been paid, he came home from work with a couple of his friends. He was supposed to take me for ice cream. I remember him leaving, telling me he was going to be back soon so we could go out. I waited for him outside until it became dark. I remember my mom yelling out the window, "Come on Keith, come in the house your father is not coming back tonight." I angrily responded that he was coming back. To make a long story short, he never did come back that night. That broke me! It did something to the trust I had in my dad. My mom tried to make me feel better, explaining that he eventually would be back and get me ice cream, just not today. I remember the anger, telling my mom that "one day dad will be old and walking with a cane and I am going to come right up and snatch that cane." Of course, my mother responded with "You do not want to do that baby, you are letting him control you and you are losing control of yourself." My mother was correct when she said I was losing control of myself. The anger I felt towards my father and the people I surrounded myself with were hiding my true self and my calling to lead. My father did come back later that night but not for long because my parents separated soon after.

A Calling to Lead

I was eighteen when I accepted Jesus Christ and two years later, I was called to preach by God. Believe me, it was not in my plan, it was not a desire of my own. Even when the calling began, I believed too many of my characteristics would disqualify me from getting into ministry. I used to stutter and stammer in my speech, so I assumed this would be a disqualification. That was my first excuse! God gave me strategies to overcome that challenge, He knew it was just a defense mechanism.

You can never disregard where you came from or think that it does not influence where you will go. That is also the truth behind the gospel, which is where I am today. The gospel envelops you. It understands your past but also seeks to regenerate and make you born again in another experience and form of development. It puts you in a better place than where you were, prior to coming to Christ.

I started to (and still do) have an insatiable desire to know more about God. After I became a Christian, I just wanted to read the Bible and learn as much as possible. In the Bible, the Apostle Peter says that when a non-believer becomes a believer, it is like how a newborn baby desires milk. As a believer, it is a desire to know the milk of God's word. That was me. I read the Bible more than I read any other book in my life. I wanted to know this God who changed my life then and continues to change my life now. The more I read, the more I wanted to know, the more I wanted to read.

At one service, I felt God was specifically talking to me. It was as if He had his finger on my chest pointing and saying, "this is where I want you to be." I went to my pastor and shared my feelings. Without hesitation, he replied, "Son, you are being called to ministry." He asked me to enroll in a theological institution. He told me that if this is what I was truly called to do, God would take care of my concerns about my job, responsibilities and needs. All I needed to do was study and share what God was saying to me with others.

I never had an epiphany, nor did I pull myself up by my own bootstraps. No one grabbed me, looked me in the eyes and told me to change. It was when I heard what Christ did to save me and the love he had for me. Christ had a love He not only talked about, but proved. God accepts and loves you as you are, not who you are meant to become. It was my turning point and I decided it was time for me to begin changing my life.

The Circle Called Life

God is a jokester, even a bit of a prankster. All that anger and distrust I had in my father helped me see my calling to God. Ultimately, it all circled back. I ended up leading my dad to Christ when I was in my mid-30s. My dad was diagnosed with cancer of the lymph nodes. When I found out, my mind flashed back to that angry conversation with my mother. It is amazing what knowing God can do for you. I no longer wanted to 'snatch that cane'. I wanted to be there for my father and help him see God's word too.

My father was living between my house and my sister's house. My sister took on a lot of responsibility when my father got sick. I wanted to be there for her as a brother and take some of that weight off my sister's shoulders. I took him to get his treatments at the Veteran's hospital. My dad looked drained and tired. I started to talk to him about his current life and his eternal destiny. As I began to share the Gospel with him, I told him I would love to be with him, in eternal life. I closed my eyes and shared that I know exactly where I am going in eternal life and that he can know the same thing. He understood and said "Yes, I want to see Christ." He stated that he did not know what he needed to do to be with the Lord and that he thought he could just be himself and that would suffice. My dad accepted Christ into his life and immediately his attitude began to change. He joined the church, sang in the male choir and was considered for a position as a church trustee.

Words of Affirmation

When my father and I finally discussed his separation from my mother, I told him that I knew the divorce was not solely his fault. He immediately became defensive saying, "No, no, no, your mother is wonderful and had no fault in this." I told my dad that I had nothing against my mother, just that I know that no couple is perfect. My mother and father both made mistakes. We all falter and fail in some way, which is why we need grace. My father began to cry. No one had ever told him the divorce was not solely his fault. The next words out of my dad's mouth were ones I will never forget. He said, "Not only are you a good preacher, good pastor and have been a great son, but you are a good man." At that moment, I did not fully grasp how profoundly important those words were to me.

It is my belief that every man needs to be affirmed, particularly from his father. In Africa, boys experience a rite of passage to adulthood. Elders may send boys out to woods to hunt or build a house and after their experience, they are viewed as men. In our society, we have no equivalence to this, which is the precise reason it is so powerful and important for a man to hear that he has made that rite of passage. That was the gift my father gave me that day.

My Father's Death

I was in my thirties when my father died. We held the service at my church. We had a member of the church who was a psychologist. She had an office in our church to support our members. One May afternoon, I passed by the office and checked in, asking how everything was going. After our short talk, she asked "How are you doing, how is your father?" I broke down and the tears poured. I was so confused, all she asked me was how my father was doing. She told me that there was something there and I needed to find the underlying cause of it. We talked for only a short while, but I felt as though we resolved so much! I missed him, and I realized his birthday was in May. She helped me work through so much of what I was feeling. She helped me recognize the power in my father's affirmation that day he told me I was a good man. I realized even with the difficulties of our relationship, I adored my father and will always work to make him proud.

An Evolving Relationship

When I was called to ministry and to gain knowledge of God, my relationships with everyone and everything began to change. My relationship with my father encouraged me to focus on the importance of my relationship with my sons. The more knowledge of God's Word I obtained, the more my relationships evolved. I am so proud of my sons. I try to instill the importance of gaining knowledge to them. I stress the significance of always having room to grow in all aspects of life, but especially in being a child of God. I want to have all conversations with my sons that my dad never had with me.

I wish the same thing for my daughters. I took my daughters on a "model" date to show them what to expect. We dressed up and went to an exquisite restaurant. More importantly, we had all the conversations about relationship expectations and the importance of God in these relationships.

All my children received a Christian K-12 education. We had a deal in my house that they had to give two years at a Christian college, and then, if they were not happy, they could transfer to a school of their liking. My wife and I wanted to support them in their formative years, give them an anchor to hold onto in the beginning of college. After that, they could make decisions as they saw fit. We did not want to be rigid with our children. We let them go to parties (of parents we knew) and listen to non-secular music. We would dissect and have intense conversations about music and interactions. We would analyze lyrics and ask what the meaning was in both a humanity perspective and divine perspective. I was not fearful about my children's actions because I trusted God and the values we had instilled in them.

I do not look for my children to be perfect. I know I am not perfect. A father's relationship with his children grows through stages. Due to my knowledge of these stages and the connection to God, I can identify the distinct stages and provide leadership when possible. Sometimes I fail. I thank God for my knowledge to have shared these stages with my children, many that my father did not share with me.

My Son's Call to Ministry

My son was also called to ministry. When it was time for him to go to college, I was encouraging him to go to Liberty University. After his second year at Liberty, he chose to live off campus with friends. He experienced the typical college life of friends, parties and drinking.

I remember the day I was about to preach at the National Baptist Convention in Philadelphia. Before my sermon, my son called. "Dad I am just so tired...of all of it." I let him talk and eventually asked him what exactly caused this feeling. He shared he was frustrated about the whole experience, the partying, the drinking. Then he said "Dad, I want to do whatever God wants me to do and I think I am being called to the ministry." I affirmed him the same way my pastor had done for me years ago. I told him about the call for knowledge and what he needed to do. I was a mentor for him throughout his journey to be a preacher. However, I focused on him being independent. He and I do not share the same style of preaching. I was the springboard for him to launch his own work and inspiration.

A Letter to Dad

Dear Dad,

I want to thank you for your consistency and showing me that you must take on responsibility when it comes to work. I want to thank you for your work ethic. I want to also thank you for the way that you expressed your love to your children. You were always affectionate, you hugged me, you kissed me on the cheek and forehead.

I want to thank you for how you liked to have fun. I just appreciate you so much. You poured so much greatness into my life and I feel lucky I can now do this for others. I am affectionate, I do not mind work and I like to have fun. I thank God for giving you to me, even the times that were negative. God worked it out for the good.

I appreciate and love you,

Keith

CHAPTER 8

—Brendon J. Jobs
"I was sad because of my father not showing interest in my life…
I was negotiating my identity."

Background/Family

My name is Brendon J. Jobs. I was born in November 1982, in Hackensack, New Jersey however I currently live in Philadelphia, PA. My mother, Yvette Barton Jobs-Atkinson is from the San Fernando Valley in Trinidad, a quaint rural region of the island. My biological father, Edward Sinclair is from Jamaica. I have limited information about my biological father because we have never met. My stepdad, Dean Jobs, who I consider my Dad, is from Port of Spain, Trinidad's capital city. *I do not refer to him as my stepfather.* He is my dad; he raised me and has always been there from as far back as I can remember. While both of my parents are from Trinidad, they met here in the United States while in college.

I am the oldest child. My brother, Quinn, is four years younger than me. My brother is my dad's biological son. My brother and I grew up together for a long time – six years, just the two of us, before my parents had two more children. My first sister, Jordan is 10 years younger than me, and my youngest sister, Nya is 17 years younger than me. My parents got so much softer by the time the girls came along. I remember having a strict upbringing. I remember watching other kids play outside while I was inside learning my multiplication tables. My sisters had a much more Montessorian upbringing in comparison filled with choices and organic lessons.

In Trinidad, Grandpa Charles, and Grandma Gloria Jobs, on my dad's side, were subjects of the British crown as part of their upbringing. They were part of the middle class, bourgeoisie. I think being raised in that type of environment affected how relationships formed in my family. My mother is from the country. She is emotional, brash, loud, feisty, and sharp in all the best and most beautifully human ways. She has an electric, fiery energy that seethes with passion. That is the dynamic of my mother's side of the family. My maternal grandmother, Helen Barton, worked at Kimble Glass factory for most of my life. She worked 16-hour shifts until her wrists and knees gave out and she could not work anymore. My grandmother could always read people well--who had a good heart, who had questionable morals. I know this skill came from the energy cultivated living in the rustic, grounded-ness of the San Fernando Valley. They are representatives of the proletariat – the working class in Trinidad and Tobago. These origins hold the kernels of how my parents can come from the same nation in the middle of the ocean, but approach life quite differently. These tensions often separate people on the island, which made their union in the United States unique and a process of complex compromise and negotiation in ways in which I am not fully aware. My siblings and me were lucky to have more than one life perspective as we matured and navigated the world---it felt like a balance. Growing up, both perspectives were helpful as we moved to several different areas in South Jersey. First, we lived in a mostly white, rural town Newfield, then moved to a mostly black town labeled urban, Pleasantville, and then back to a majorly white town, Galloway Township. My parents provided me with a balance of personalities to draw from, build character and cultivate experiences.

My biological father's name is Edward Sinclair. He is almost 20 years older than my mother. To my knowledge, I do not believe my biological father was involved in my life at all, in terms of supporting my mother or getting to know me. I do not remember when I officially heard about him but can faintly remember my grandmother Helen speaking of him. It felt like a family secret that only I knew about. I experienced hurt, and feelings of abandonment because I did not have time with him. I felt as though he did not want to see or know me. I am still learning how to release some of that anger and confusion. After I graduated from college in New York City, I moved into my first apartment in West Philadelphia. By that point, I had confronted my mother with the information that I knew about Edward and wanted to learn more about him. With love and understanding, my mother gave me his contact information and I worked up the courage to make initial contact--a phone call.

When I first spoke with Edward, I remember feeling overcome with emotion. Since then, we have spoken five or six times, yet only developed a limited relationship if even that. He has a family which means I have half siblings and a stepmother whom I have never met and likely never will. I learned that my biological father is a carpenter, speaks multiple languages and grew up in Jamaica before emigrating to Tea Neck, New Jersey in the 1970s, well before my birth. Apparently, I also have relatives on his side who instead of leaving Jamaica for the United States chose London and other parts of the United Kingdom. I have so many questions but could sense during each call that he limited the amount of himself he would share with me. Despite my excitement, Edward was not very forthcoming when I suggested we meet in person. We chose dates and he would cancel, leaving me with nothing but my unanswered questions. What traits did I inherit from my father? I wanted to know the good, bad, and ugly. Have I inherited any patterns of thinking from him? Perhaps, we share mannerisms and characteristics I do not have with anyone else.

My mother and biological father were never married, and never lived together. My mother came to the United States when she was 16 years old. When she was 18, she enrolled in school at Fairleigh Dickinson College, now Dickinson University. My mother makes it a point to always talk about how much joy she felt when I was born in a way that reminds me how deep her love is for me. I was born into a tribe of people who were excited to have me. When I asked her the story of my name, she shared that when she learned I would be a boy, she began looking in baby naming books. She found "Brendon" means *Prince*, and her search was over. My mom has never shared how she met Edward, how their relationship transpired or why he disappeared. I do not know if I really want all the details. My mother did not think about how hard, scary, and lonely it would be to raise a child alone. She was joyful for my arrival and prepared to provide me the best upbringing she could in a new country. Years later, she met Dean Jobs and they began cultivating a family influenced by their own upbringings.

Physical Appearance/Characteristics

I do not know who I look like. I have never met my biological dad. I have seen one or two pictures of him. People (like my grandmother) say I look like him. I think I look like my mom.

Father's teachings and career

My Dad, Dean Jobs was my role model. He taught me how to navigate school and earn a living. His example complimented what I learned from my mother. While my brother and I were growing up, he was an adjunct professor of Computer Science at Atlantic County Community College. When we were young, he trained us to code programming languages like RPG/400 and AS/400, and would take us to his introductory-level classes at the college. I learned so much about seeing a Black man lead a space without fully realizing the impact that it would have on me later in life. I was in complete awe of him and it widened the possibilities I could imagine for myself. My Dad is reflective, but somewhat hesitant about openly sharing his emotions. He guards his thoughts and feelings and they must be pulled out of him. In my life, I have noticed this reticence as a pattern of masculinity, and I try not to follow suit.

In the 1980s, my dad made a career as a computer programmer in Atlantic City during the casino boom. Soon after, he set up his own consulting business. I remember watching him grow his own client base, working from home. My dad would always tell me, "Brendon, you want to be your own boss. You do not want to work for anybody. You do not want to be indebted to anybody." This showed me the level of confidence my father possessed. It was this confidence that supported me in the tough decisions I made in my career. This experience ultimately helped me make the leap to start a consulting business of my own.

Lessons Learned

I need to work on healing from the *lessons* I learned from my biological father. Not having him around growing up and the limited access I have had to him in my adulthood makes me feel as though I cannot depend on people. I do not want that to be true. One must depend on others to truly live in a community that is healing, collective and encouraging. Isolation thrives on distance, both spatial and emotional. I believe in the power of collective community, but I have been affected by human selfishness. I often feel I am unable to fully gauge the wholeness of my own reflection or personhood because of Edward's evasiveness. My own mirror is missing foundational components given the distance and dissonance that exists in my relationship with my biological father. I have learned how difficult it is to define myself through the reflection in someone else's mirror.

Relationship with parents and grandparents

I was closest to my maternal grandmother, Helen Barton. Because my mother had me when she was so young, Helen took a significant hand in raising me. My mother was young, new to this country and trying to make a way for herself and me. I spent a lot of time at my Mum-Mum's house, with aunts and uncles who were close in age. They felt like my siblings. Each weekend, I begged my mother to bring me to my grandmother's house to spend the night. We were growing up together in rural New Jersey (Vineland, New Jersey). Helen had the most wonderful sense of humor and always reminded me to laugh. What good medicine. She had a great energy, similar in many ways to my mother.

My paternal grandmother, Gloria Jobs was a head teacher at an all-boys school in Port of Spain, Trinidad. We were not close. I learned a lot from her poise, thoughtfulness, and strength. I never really felt close to her but always wanted to know her better. Perhaps the distance was because she knew the truth, that my dad was not my biological father. I wonder still whether that created a distance between me and her in a way that never existed between her and my younger brother.

My relationship with my mother has grown exponentially. When you grow up, you think your parents know everything, but growing up, everything felt uncertain. There was tension between my mother and me especially in my adolescent years as I grappled with my own sexuality and racial identity development. My mother always told me, "I am your mother, not your friend." Now, I know that those boundaries provided me security and limits. Now we have a deeply affectionate friendship. I call my mom, just to check in and ask her about her day. This developed over time. She is my only family member who reaches out to me without me having to reach out first. I feel like I am always reaching out to my family. My mom always reminds me of my importance in this world.

I feel deeply indebted to Dean Jobs for cultivating in me a sense of intellectual curiosity about society, especially about what it means to be Black man in this world, a black man who is not African American, who is a part of the greater Black diaspora. He piqued my interest in that area early in my childhood. He is the son of an educator. He is a computer scientist. He is also a radically well-read, professorial questioner of everything. He takes pride in being deeply black, and "Trini to da bone." I have always admired those aspects of him; and have worked to make them pieces of me. While he is not my biological father, he is my Dad, and as a child, these beliefs were all encompassing. My dad is only two years older than my mother. When I reflect on the task he took on as his own of raising me, I am forever grateful. My dad married young and took on grown man responsibilities without a sense of duty and purpose.

My parents divorced when I was in college. I think my youngest sister Nya was probably the most affected, forced to grow up traveling back and forth between two homes in Galloway and Atlantic City. When they divorced, I had developed a relationship with my mother to the point that I just wanted her to be happy and at peace. I learned a lot following the separation– thinking about how short a moment we have on earth. It is important to find fulfillment within that moment. There was tension between my dad and me, in terms of how to maneuver the relationship that had changed between my parents. I remember years when we would have to figure out which child went to which parent's house for Thanksgiving dinner and a host of other holiday negotiations. In British style, I have no recollection of any explosive arguments. There was an absence of talking about what we were feeling or experiencing. The silence of not being able to be honest about how the change was affecting us as a family was uncomfortable. There was a year or two where I spoke exclusively to my mother. This was the result of my refusal to reach out to anyone who was not reaching out to me. Petty, I know, but at the time it felt like emotional self-preservation. I was in my 20s, busy with the super important everyday business of life. Today, I feel like I am reaching out more to my dad. When I do, I love our conversations. Our relationship is different from my relationship with my mom. My mother and I talk about cooking, society, what we are feeling, and family. My dad and I talk about the world, blackness and a lot about work.

I hope it is God's plan for me to get to know Edward Sinclair and Dean Jobs as deeply as possible. I do not put out enough effort to get to know Dean Jobs. I should call more and am not sure what holds me back. I am not putting out that effort with either one of them. I guess part of me is still in that petty mode, if they choose not to reach out to me then, why should I reach out to them? I do not care, except I do. I am trying to emotionally work through this issue. It is simplistic to assume that someone not reaching equates to them not caring about me. I think in some ways my not reaching out is because of the fear of rejection. I have felt that pain before. They have not said it openly to me. I often imagine that if I do take the risk and reach out, I will feel/believe they did not want to hear from me. When I call Edward Sinclair, he rarely answers, nor returns my calls. In many ways, this diminishes my feeling of self-worth. It should not be that way, since it is obvious that the issue is with him and not with me. Nonetheless, it still stings. Dean Jobs answers my calls or returns them if I leave a message. I always feel better after we speak.

In the past, I resented both my biological father and stepdad. I was bitter toward Dean Jobs because he was emotionally distant. He worked so much and missed my activities. I do not harbor that resentment toward him anymore. I do feel a palpable sadness when I think of Edward Sinclair. I wish for a perfect father-son relationship versus what exists. A pattern of thought prevents me from calling, because he probably has no interest in hearing from me. Whether true or not, it is something I frequently replay in my inner dialogue. I think this belief system limits the potential for relationships to be meaningful. Who knows what they might be carrying, and not talking about that limits the depth of relationships I have with them? I feel they have both lived through hardships they choose not to discuss. Dean Jobs shares stories that are light and often funny. I have no access to the profound disappointment he had to navigate or manage in his life as Black man working as a professional in a racist society. It makes me angry that he lives with this disappointment, because I have seen how hard he has worked to make sure he provided for his family. I hope to have more access to that; I cannot be angry because I know that what he had to do was difficult beyond measure. I am experiencing my own form of hardship. With Edward, I wish he would just speak with me. I do not know what he is afraid of, or what he thinks I want. Why can we not just talk? There is always a barrier. Resentment eats away at a person slowly, so I continue to try to let go. I fear he will pass away before I can get the answers, I feel I need to bring me some form of emotional satisfaction or closure. I wonder whether his other children have that access. I do not know if this type of openness is even part of his personality.

I was sad because of my father not showing interest in my life. My family did not know; I did not talk about it. I would cry about it, a profound, deep cry – there were days I could not hold on to those emotions anymore. I remember the paper I had with his number scribbled on it. I felt like I was missing out. I have always thought that my brother was lucky because he knew where he came from, who his dad was and what he represented. Why was I not enough to know my biological dad?

I would like to get to know my biological father so that I can learn about my lineage, where I am from, where I am going. I think I am building a future that leaves me endlessly curious. I do not have a full sense of what it means to be grounded and I feel a relationship with him would change this for me. This is my *wow* card. I do not even know if I am going to lose my hair. I do not know what he looks like, his siblings? My siblings? Developing a relationship with him would give me the missing puzzle piece, and possibly see what my future holds.

I think of the phrase, *be careful what you wish for…*what if he had been around? Would my life be different? Worse? The dreamer in me imagines flying to Sweden to meet my uncle or trips to see family in London or Jamaica. I do not know. I cannot say. Maybe, he was protecting me?

I have not experienced abuse. I have gotten my ass whipped and deserved it. We see more corporal punishment in black families. I like what Dr. Joy DeGruy says about this phenomenon in *Post-Traumatic Slave Syndrome*. She explains that our ancestors were punished by 'the whip' as slaves. This has replicated patterns and caused many black households to embrace something that was not necessarily meant for good. In many ways, I grew up in a traditional black household. I feel like I have been fully encultured.

Struggles

I did not see my mother struggle because of my biological father. She never spoke about him. I did not feel like I was missing much. It was always something whispered. It is a fact of the family, not one in need of further examination. I am not sure it needs further scrutiny. My stepdad supported us all, in a way of being there physically, intellectually, and spiritually. The emotional connection – I think that was a space where he modeled his behavior around what he saw as a child.

Music/Cultural Influences

My mom and dad were always clear to remind us (my brother and me), "When you leave the house you are walking into Galloway Township, but when you close the door, I do not care what you think, this is Trinidad." When that door closes this is Trinidad. Do not imagine that you have any rights or liberties." We would always compare ourselves to other children. Cultural influences permeated throughout our home, including food. We did not eat out or eat fast food. We did not have much money. My dad was great at managing finances. He was austere and bought what we needed and nothing more. We ate curry chicken, goat and roti when we could get it. If we were lucky enough to go to Brooklyn to see family, we would get pholourie and Trini goodies, such as tamarind balls.

Music influences our culture. I think about the Mighty Sparrow, who my mother and grandmother loved. Bob Marley is a giant for the culture. I need jazz to set my energy. I like to sing. I love instruments and memorizing music. I play six instruments. I began playing the flute in second grade. In third or fourth grade, another student was playing the clarinet, and I liked the number of buttons, so I began playing. It has remained my primary instrument, I played through high school, and became the first chair in my high school's concert band. I also played in the All-New Jersey Band. The clarinet was not a marching instrument and had similar fingering to other instruments. Mr. Dondero, my music teacher, told me it has similar fingering to the saxophone and encouraged me to play. I began playing the tenor saxophone. When it was time for me to start marching, I did not want to march with the clarinet. The band director told me about the mellophone, an upright French horn. That was a leap and took a bit of time to learn. Eventually, I became section leader of the mellophone group for the marching band. Then, I began to master the French horn. I also learned how to play the trumpet. My favorite instrument was the clarinet. I preferred singing more, it felt more spiritual. I could hear a song and sing it. It took a lot of practice to perform well with instruments.

I love black female singers. I love gospel music, which it is a deviation from my family. My family is not religious. I was the only one who went to church.

Trinidad Experiences

During the summer, my brother and I went home to Trinidad to stay with Grandma Gloria and Grandpop Chalo (Charles). During the summer of 1992, due to a coupe, we were trapped in Trinidad. There were no planes coming in or leaving. I remember men with huge guns, curfews at night, gunshots in the hills. We went to my grandmother's school. We got a dose of what it meant to be a student in the Trinidadian context. It was brutal. They beat you. I remember playing a game of Round Robin, where you compete with a child to say a times table faster than another student. I have always been slow with math. I would lose the game. The teacher would paddle the loser. My brother refused to nap in kindergarten, so the teachers beat him until he napped. There is an interesting culture of corporal punishment, with the intent on emphasizing the school's mission and purpose. School was not a place to find yourself but spaces to build yourself up enough to make your ancestry proud. While we were there, we did not see my mother's family much. There was about an hour of travel time between Port of Spain and the San Fernando Valley, and we never slept over.

Favorite Sitcoms/Movies

We loved "In Living Color". In Trinidad, there were only two television channels. My mother sent us video recordings of shows we enjoyed. The tape had the Simpsons, In Living Color, 227, and The Cosby Show. We also had a tape we watched many times of The Color Purple. I did not realize the queer back story between Shug Avery and Miss Ceily but it was why I loved the movie.

When I got back to the States, I liked Martin. I was fascinated with Black American culture, more than I was with Black Trini Culture. Growing up, I bathed myself in black American culture as I returned to attend my largely segregated school in Pleasantville, New Jersey.

Mother's Career

My mother did not finish college. My brother and I were born four years apart. At the same time, there was a huge casino boom in New Jersey. My mother was an executive slot host. Part of her role was to identify high rollers and recruit them to specific properties. My mom was a people person. She is an extrovert, beautiful, charismatic, and good at shapeshifting to navigate complex social situations. It always seemed like she could talk to anyone. Growing up, I was very shy. I spoke through my instruments. My mother would put on her Donna Karen suits and go to work. I grew up with Black Girl Magic. There was not a name for it then. I was so proud of her. There were emotional and physical costs to it too. I think the stress was part of the cost, being a Black woman in a racist environment. I know she bore a cost from it. At one point, she got a stomach ulcer from the stress. She worked swing shifts. My Grandma Helen worked for Kimmel Glass factory (18-hour shifts). My mother was doing a similar hustle. I found my mother's career more appealing to me. When she was pregnant with my youngest sister (1999), she stepped away from it and recalibrated her goals.

Mentorship

I have been lucky enough to have the guidance, influence, and support of Dr. Howard Stevenson from *Lion's Story*. He provides profound support and advice regarding my path. When I reach out to him, he responds. I get excited when he responds, the same way I feel when my dad responds. He is a part of my village. Speaking with him gives me the profound confidence and responsibility to move forward with professional decisions. Having this mentorship relationship with this Black man, makes me think about the depth of my relationships with my biological and stepdad.

Education

My favorite teacher was Ms. Lakins, my 5th grade teacher in Pleasantville, NJ. This is a black school district. Right before puberty, I was playing double-Dutch with the girls. During this time, I was teased by the girls, and bullied by the boys. After an incident where I was punched in the face, Ms. Liken decided to have lunch with me every day. She took her personal time to give me a safe space. She created an atmosphere for me where I felt loving care. I never thought I could feel that in school. I spoke with her last year, over 25 years since I was a student in her class; she is a counselor now. I thank her to this day for it because I do not know where I would be without having that safety net when I needed it most.

I feel I have been well- educated. I hated K-12 school; I did it out of a sense of duty, and I did it well. I was not interested in schoolwork but completed it thoroughly. I went to school to be in the band. I relied on music to get me through school. Especially in Galloway Township, the mostly white school district, my English and history classes were places of profound oppression. No one seemed to care about the blackness in school; I was being socialized to not care about it, because that was how you earned high grades. The only time Black people existed were as slaves, servants, or victims and my school community felt quietly comfortable with the reality they created. I just wanted to get to college so I could be done with school.

When I was younger, the idea of going to college was not about the educational experience or connecting with the community. It was about "the stuff" I would have because of going to college – capitalism.

From 2001-2005, I attended Columbia University. It was there that I realized how short life is, and how quickly it can change. As a result of the September 11th bombing, I began studying international relations, the idea of the nation's state, because I did not know why this was happening. I began looking at the idea of race relations, other ways of organizing ourselves. I dug into race relations. This was when I had my first black male educator, Winston James, who taught the course, *Race and Color in America*. He shattered everything I had learned during my primary years, and still has me questioning and journeying today. I was amazed that he critically challenged white people to their faces. I had never seen this done before, and with such confidence! I wanted to be able to do the same.

I applied to law school. Before I decided to enroll, I wanted to make sure I really wanted to follow that path. I decided to apply to Teach for America, was accepted into the program and then kicked out shortly thereafter. At that time, I needed a lot of support as a black male in an educational space where children were not accustomed to seeing black men in leadership roles. Teach for America was not equipped to mentor me in that space. They had not yet confronted the fact that their model was built upon a foundation of white supremacy culture that encouraged white savior practices. I regularly heard fellow members make disparaging remarks about the school communities that were signing up to teach which also diminished my value as a burgeoning black male educator.

I began working at a law firm. They had new cars, fancy homes worth showing off, and took vacations where they traveled abroad. But people appeared to be unhappy. I experienced covert racism, tokenization and marginalization in this space and decided that this was not the best path for me.

I returned to the classroom and began teaching at the Philadelphia High School for Girls. That helped me think about where I wanted to go. I taught Black history, as part of the new requirement in public schools. That space also led me to questioning gender, patriarchy, and power dynamics around gender. I began graduate school at the University Pennsylvania – the teaching learning curriculum program. We studied how gender can impact classroom performance. We discussed how to create intrinsic motivation. I am wondering if I need a doctorate to continue my work in this path. My financial status is a true inhibitor for me pursuing a doctorate. I see the ceiling and connect with my Dad's experience as it relates to this matter. I see humanity in this aspect without him having to explicitly speak his heart here because I am now familiar with the limitations that Blackness puts on professional opportunities in America. I try to make school an equitable place for children.

Sexuality

When I was 16, people began asking me about my future. I remember responding "I do not know. I just want to have a Benz wagon for all of my babies." However, at the time I would make these responses, I knew I was gay.

In the 1990's, I was quiet about my sexuality. I did my best to fit into the "man box." I did not come out until I was 17 years old. I told my parents when I was coming home from college for Christmas. They were disappointed. At the time, I felt it; I do not feel it now. I think my parents knew. The internal struggle was mine. The memory of that conversation with my parents is fuzzy. I remember seeing blue walls. They said, "we love you just as you are, and of course you can come home for Christmas." I was able to have this conversation with distance. I would briefly go home for holidays, see my family, and then quickly return to my cocoon in New York. While I was in college, I was negotiating my identity. My parents never said they were disappointed, but my mother wanted me to have children. She has a grandchild from my brother. When you have a queer child, things shift. I do not know if it is fictional. I want to honor it as being possible. I felt it somewhere. Now, when I visit Trinidad, I am with family. I am not a part of the queer community.

I believe that people are born with these affinities. For me personally, I feel I was born this way. Before puberty, my queer identity had nothing to do with my attraction to other people. It had to do with playing barbie dolls, an attraction to the feminine esthetic. This was all before puberty. After puberty, I realized it was not about just esthetic affinities, but how I like to form relationships with humans. I like to form relationships and connect with men. I do not feel nor look for this type of connection with women. That is not my attraction. I think I was born, with and have grown into this identity. But now, as an adult, I realize that I am part of a community and do not stand alone. We share a way of growing up, living, and relating to the world.

When I was in ninth grade, I had a girlfriend –Patience Etim. Patience and I were both immigrant children and in the marching band together. Her family is from Nigeria. We were in the marching band together. Also, I took a girl to the junior prom and ended up skipping senior prom. By then, I had lost interest in attempting to fit myself into societal norms around sex and sexuality.

Religion

I was the only one who went to church in my family. My Dad's grandmother was Catholic and religious. She was a teacher leader. She would take her family several times a week. That turned my dad off from the church. I also think there were teachings and beliefs in the Seven Day Adventist Church that my mother did not agree with, so by the time they had children, they did not want to raise us in the church.

When I initially wanted to go, the music (choir, bands, drums) and the connection with the people drew me to the church. Being around

White cultures in schools, the church was a black space that felt like mana (food from the Gods). It felt like life.

I would not consider myself a strong man of faith. I consider faith to be beyond rationality. Faith is something you rely on when you cannot or do not want to explain something. I would describe myself more spiritual than faith-based or rooted in any one church. There is a middle ground, where I connect to who I am in this moment. I am not here alone but in a line of people that go back beyond what I can trace. I have an intense relationship to the energy connected to my existence on the planet, in my house, and in the environments I visit. Energy reverberates when we walk into a space. It can be a light or dark energy. I do have faith in something higher. I call out to Jesus, because of my Christian upbringing. I wonder if the community that embraced me was not Christian, would I be calling out to those deities? I believe in prophets, but I also believe in spirituality.

Depiction of a Man

I think about the binary. I think about media stereotypes. I think about the "man-box", limited, driven by sports and talk of what we are doing and not how we are feeling, heterosexuality, as what should be and what is, without deviation. I think about living in contradiction to the man box by allowing myself to experience and share a robust range of emotions.

As a queer black man, the depiction of a man is broader. I think about a human being, first, who has a lot of work to do with emotions. Men have so much work to do with emotions, because there are so many contradictions that come when we show them to others. We must defend ourselves against judgements if we have long hair, or wear colors that are generally feminine.

When I think about a two-parent household, I think there is the *Leave it to Beaver* version, filled with time, attention, love, care, dinner around the table, family outings, and conversations about what happened in school. Mine was not like that. It was a working house. I was working on my instruments and schoolwork. My siblings were doing the same. My mom was working outside the house, and when she was home, she was exhausted. My dad was working in the house. We were all working to keep the house clean. There was a lot of work, but not a lot of connection. We were connected because we lived in the same space and shared cultural values. We were a tribe of people together. But I think a two-parent household does not necessarily feel connected.

Letter to Dad

Dear "Dad,"

Thank you for life. I am having an enjoyable time with this. Life has been, so far, rich, and profound, filled with people, love, and experiences. I have been able to connect with people in places and ways that I think would make our ancestors proud.

Growing up did not feel easy, but I wonder if growing up feels easy for anyone. I wonder sometimes if the feeling of growing up would have been easier if you were around. I wonder if you were protecting me by not being around.

But mostly, I just wonder about you.

Love,

Brendon

CHAPTER 9

—Reginald Day
"I remember thinking, where is Dad?
Why is he not here to help us?"

Background

My name is Reginald Day and I live in Philadelphia, Pennsylvania. I do not think I will ever live in another city. I was born and raised in North Philadelphia. My mother is from Philly and my father is from Baltimore. My parents met when my father moved to Philadelphia from Baltimore. I was born in 1977, at Jefferson Hospital in Center City, Philadelphia. Interestingly, I was never supposed to be here. I had an older sister who passed away a few days after her birth. If that was not painful enough, the doctors told my mother she would never be able to have more children, but God had other plans. My parents spoiled me. I was an only child, and they gave me everything I needed and tried to provide everything I wanted.

I believe I have facial features of both of my parents. I think I have my father's nose and maybe his smile. As for my likeness to my mother, I would have to say the eyes. But if you see me around my father, you will know that I am his child. I find comfort in knowing when people see me, they see my father.

Character and a Father's Love

When I think of my similarities to my mother, I think of my character. My mother is there for everyone. She has a warmness about her, especially around children. When you see me around children, you can tell that some of my mother's warmness rubbed off on me. I did not inherit that personality trait from my father. It is strange observing his warmth and love around my daughter, his grandchild. The observation is foreign to me; I was not shown this type of love when I was a child. The father I remember was stern. My daughter is receiving the love, laughter, and fun I was missing. It appears he is trying to avoid the same mistake when he is with my daughter. Through her, my father is showing me that there is love, laughter, and fun.

An Absent Role

My father did not spend much time with me. I know my mother was fielding questions "Mom, where is Dad?" and sugar coating it with "Oh, he is just taking care of something." When I was three years old, my mother and father divorced, and shared custody began. My father would pick me up on the weekends when he had the time. He would take me to my aunt's house, let me be around family, but it really was not the quality time I wanted and needed from my father. I think this is where I really began to feel the absence of my father. I began to question if the role and responsibility of fatherhood was something he really wanted.

As I got older, I stopped questioning the whereabouts of my father. I became accustomed to life being just my mom and me. There were times where my father would say that he was coming to see me and would not show. With each lie, I became more comfortably uncomfortable. I had no interest in knowing why this was happening or what issue remained unresolved. Sadly, the neglect became commonplace.

In grade school, I remember my peers always talking about what their dads did for work. I only spoke about my mother. My mother worked for U.S. Customs. For a black family, this was considered a respectable job because it was steady, consistent, and considered an acceptable living. I had no interest in sports like the other boys in my class. My mother and I did not discuss sports or go outside to play basketball on the weekends. I never asked my mom to be part of a club, sports teams, or anything because I watched her struggling with all the responsibilities that fell on only her shoulders.

I attended a Catholic grade school and had many friends in the neighborhood. However, it was a different story when I went to high school. I attended a Roman Catholic, all-boys, diverse high school. Looking back, it was high school where I really needed my dad to be present. I started getting into mischief and made some poor choices in my attempt to figure out how to become a man. It was hard to speak to my mother about certain subjects. I felt uncomfortable talking to her about fighting, girls or sex. I wanted to talk to my dad, but unfortunately, he was not around to help. I started to look towards other people in my life who could fill the void my dad created. At that age, my role models were the "hustlers," the people who were in the street, independent and free from rules and regulations. I would see them with money, girls, and nice cars. That was who I wanted to emulate. So, I turned to them to ask what I needed to do to build myself up, as a man.

The divorce happened when I was so young it is almost like I really had not noticed. The separation between me and my father grew slowly. It was not until my dad remarried that the separation that had grown became noticeable. Now I was sharing my dad with his new wife and her children. It became a clear separation of my mom and me on one side and my father and his new family on the other.

I felt abandoned, neglected, and betrayed. I began to shelter myself, refusing to show emotion toward anyone. Life hurt less when I put myself in an emotionless bubble. I did not want my friends to know about my dad and I never wanted to hear about their dads. I felt insecure talking about my life, I always felt like there was so much I did not know and never wanted others to think I was unintelligent.

My Mother's Struggles

When my father moved out, my mother had to take on the responsibility of raising a child on her own. She worked extremely hard to make sure I had everything I needed but I know it was tough for her. Bills started coming in, she had to pay rent on her own and she wanted to ensure I had a good education. When she decided to go back to school to earn more money, I could see the struggle. Most days she would work early mornings to late nights, with an hour bus ride both ways. Sometimes I would stay with my aunt so my mother could work or complete assignments for school.

Music's Impact

In my mother's home, I was not allowed to listen to anything but gospel music. Both my mother's and father's families were big in the church. I did it all, every choir, bible study, prayer meeting, you name it, I did it. Church was in me before I was in church.

At my aunt's house, I was able to be a little more rebellious. I listened to music that, really, I should not have been listening to and that my mother would never allow. I started hearing N.W.A., Run DMC, LL Cool J, and other well-known rappers.

Three Unknown Brothers

My father was married previously before he met my mother. I have three brothers that I recently met. I met my first brother unexpectedly at a Thanksgiving dinner in 2014! My father told us all he had to make a run and would be back shortly. When he returned, another man was with him. When I met him, I could tell we were related but had no clue he was my brother. It was then I was told my two other brothers had unreconciled issues with my dad and refused to meet me. That is not the case and now. I have a good relationship with my brothers. Two of the three I communicate with regularly. The other brother and I are still trying to bond. We speak, we have each other's phone number, but we do not communicate as much as we could. I am starting to build more of a connection with my estranged brothers now and that is because we are talking more frequently. I am genuinely happy that we are learning so much about each other and the father we share. We are sharing personal stories and experiences. Interestingly, we are all in search of answers. It feels nice to have established these connections. I believe that they are dealing with similar feelings of neglect and abandonment.

When I graduated high school, my relationship with my father improved. When I was younger my father spent more time with my older cousins than me. Through them, he heard about my accomplishments. It was during my first year in college that my father began to have more of a presence in my life. This is how my relationship with my father began to improve. As I got older, I had more access to my father. He also treated me as an adult and I was privy to a lot of dialogue that was hidden in my younger years. One day, he was talking to me as if I knew I had three brothers. Yeah, I talked to your brother today." I remember immediately thinking "What brother?" He went on talking about a man named Joe (which is my father's name) until finally I asked, "Who is Joe?" It was then I learned that not only was Joe my brother, but I had two other brothers, Marshall, and Bill.

As time passed, I realized that it was not that my father did not want to tell me about my brothers, but he could not, as, like me, he had almost no relationship with them. He had no answers about them, their lives or how they were doing. I believe that was why my father was starting to build a relationship with just me. He was coming to realize that he had four sons and did not know much about any of them.

I do not blame my mom for not nurturing a relationship between myself and my brothers. Certain things I think my father should have told me. It was not my mother's responsibility to tell me about my father's earlier marriage. My mom only shared that he had been previously married.

The Robbery

When I was ten years old, my mother and I lived in a rough area. One day, my mother came home, and noticed someone had broken into our house. They stole our VCR and some other items. At the time, I was at my grandfather's house and she called to have me come home. During that time in my life, I stayed with my grandfather after school until my mother came home from work. When I arrived, I saw the police and the side door open and was confused. My mom explained that we had been robbed but everything would be fine. I felt a bit lost and my mother suggested I go outside and play with my friends. Later that evening when I returned home, I called for my mother. She did not answer me. I finally found her in her bedroom, on her knees, crying over the Bible saying, "Thank you Lord, thank you Lord, thank you Lord." I knew not to interrupt. I went to my room and did everything in my power to block out her voice. Soon after, my mom told me, "God is about to do something in our lives. So just be prepared." I thought my mother had lost her mind. I could not figure out what she was trying to tell me or how I could make the situation better. I remember thinking *where is Dad? Why is he not here to help us?* There was nothing I could do. I tried to make a plan to protect us. I was too young to buy a gun. I debated if we should get a dog, or if I should just sit by the door, all day, every day. All I owned was a whiffle ball bat, but I decided that was enough. I planned to sit by the door and if a burglar tried to rob us again, I would hit him with my bat. After the burglary, I always entered the house first. To this day, when I help my mother, I remember the fear I felt after the burglary and not being able to protect her.

My Own Struggles

I never consistently attended classes during my first year of college. I was following in the paths of my role models, gambling, playing cards and looking for ways to make quick money. It became a cycle. I would be in class; someone would mention playing cards and I would leave. It was like an addiction. My then-girlfriend would take notes for me, so I was passing, but I was always gambling. Life continued to go downhill. I started hanging around drug dealers and guys from the block. I had family and close friends who sold drugs and although they never let me, they paid me to stand around the block and be a lookout for police officers. At the time, I felt like this was what I was supposed to be doing. This is what my role models were doing. If I wanted to be a man and have the money and the women, this was it. I still had a 'real job' at a pharmacy but as soon as I was off, it was back to the block.

I eventually dropped out of college. I was honest with my mom and told her all I was doing in college was gambling. Her response, "Well then you are getting a job." I got a job doing security for The University of the Arts. It was nothing like my pharmacy job, it took a lot of my time. They really looked out for me, I had benefits, extra shifts and they saw my potential. Suddenly, I did not have time to be hanging out on the corner, I had to really work. I saw friends arrested, jailed or killed. That life was no longer for me.

From 2002-2008, I became a Philadelphia Police Officer. I was a regular beat cop. I had a certain area that I patrolled-ironically, a high drug area. I was able to work as a plain clothes officer until I got into a scary situation, while working undercover on a burglary detail. I called for backup. When police arrived, they could not see my badge and were unaware I was undercover. They drew their guns, and I could have been killed. After that, I felt that it was time for me to stop working undercover. I stayed in uniform for the rest of my career.

I Became the Protector My Mother Needed

I did not want to be a police officer. I ran security for several years with different organizations. A friend of mine and my Godbrother became police officers. They both pushed me to take the police exam, even though at the time, I really did not want anything to come of it. I was not called to interview for a position until almost two years after I had taken the exam. I had forgotten all about it- I thought they were calling me to interview me about a crime. I remember thinking "Whatever you think I did; I did not do it." Turns out, they wanted to interview me for a job. Ultimately, the decision was based on finances. Becoming a police officer came with higher pay, better benefits, and security. I wanted to serve the community and help children to feel safe and protected. I went into schools to ensure the school safety was correct and patrolled several recreational and community events to ensure the protection of everyone, especially children.

Characteristics of my Father

My father was a 'fix-it yourself' type of person. He never called anyone to help him, he just got it done. That is a quality I inherited. I am the go-to person in the family and I will always try to fix something myself before I call anyone else.

My father taught me to be an enterprising person. I have never seen my father not working. Even when my father was laid off from his job, he never stopped being a hustler. He was always putting up a fence for somebody, building a wall or painting a house. He was the person others went to when they needed help. I get that from him, I am the go-to person.

I always said I would never be like my father when I had a child. I was going to marry the woman who had my child and be there every step of the way. That did not happen. Do not get me wrong, I am a huge part of my daughter's life, but I did not marry my daughter's mother. While I am not blaming this rocky relationship on my father, I cannot help but think about how I saw myself possessing many of the same qualities. It is one

111

of the reasons I never asked my mom why they separated- because deep down I already knew, he cheated, and my mother caught him.

Now, I believe it is so important for me to recognize and learn from my mistakes. My daughter is eight years old. She needs a role model for how women should be treated and she deserves respect.

Ending a Cycle

My daughter is now growing up in a single parent household. She lives with her mother, but our co-parenting is nothing like my parents had with me. My daughter is with me several days per week and her mom and I work together to set a good example. We go to events for her together, like parent teacher conferences, and everyone assumes we are together. My daughter and I pray every night. My mom has her involved in the church just like I was when I was younger. I think because of how well her mom and I work together, my daughter does not feel different from others because her parents separated. She is open about it in school, telling others, "I have two houses, my dad's and my mom's."

Relationships

Relationships are rough for me. My mother remained single after my dad. She never remarried, there was never anyone around the house and I never had a stepfather. So, when it came to relationships, I learned from my cousin, who is now deceased. I watched how he acted in relationships, most of them being long-term. I aspired to have long term relationships, but I also liked to have fun. At one time, I was a party promoter. It was my job to talk to girls and if I was in a relationship, that usually did not go well. Back then, I did not see why my job as a party promoter always affected my relationships. In my mind, I was bringing in money and it was my job. I did not stop and think about how it might be hurting my relationship or that I actually needed to address the problems.

To this day I do not think I have ever been "in love." When I think of my parent's relationship, my aunt's boyfriend who beat her, and other people in my life, I could tell what was *not* love. I do not believe I ever seen examples of two people in love when I was young.

I witnessed how my cousins protected my aunt when her boyfriend assaulted her. They immediately confronted him about the physical abuse. I remember walking down the street with my aunt once and a guy 'cat-calling' her. I immediately went over and kicked him. It was all I knew to do; my cousins were not there, and I needed to protect my aunt.

My Father's Wedding

When my father remarried, I did not receive an invitation to the wedding. I knew he had a new girlfriend, but I found out about his wedding through my mom. He called my mom and said, "I got married yesterday." I can remember blocking it out as usual because it was my "go to" so I did not have to feel the sadness of what came along with his decisions. Now my father's wife (my stepmom) and I get along great. We have a terrific relationship and talk often.

Three Adjectives to Describe My Father

Courageous. My dad had much to overcome. He grew up in Baltimore, Maryland and moved to Philadelphia. He faced prejudice growing up. He worked for the sanitation department and did everything he could to put food on the table.

Dedicated. My dad has always shown his dedication to his siblings. He will always take care of my aunts and uncles. From stories I have heard, he has always been that way, even though he is not the oldest child. That hurt me because he was never that way to me, his own son. However, it gave me a quality to try to emulate. I want to make sure my family looks to me as the person that will always support them.

Loving. Growing up, it was difficult for my dad to show love. Anytime my dad said "I love you" it was short and felt meaningless. Now, I believe my dad has learned how to love and how to express love, making it more meaningful, by providing hugs and words about why he loves me.

A Letter to My Father

Dear Dad,

I know our relationship has not always been easy. There are questions I have and answers I need. I forgive you for when you were not there for me. I appreciate all you have done in my life and know our relationship has improved. I wish the best for you in all you do. You are still my dad, my father. You continue to lift me up when I struggle. You showed me how to embrace a talent with my hands that has been extremely resourceful. After having conversations with you, I learned why you are the way you are and do what you do. I forgive you for all the wrong. I ask that we continue to build our relationship. Be the father that I know you can be. I ask you to help me understand all that confuses me. I hope that we can get past the rough times and clear any confusion from past events. I thank you for being the grandfather that you are to Londyn. I thank you for opening and sharing what you have with me. Simply, I thank you for just being you.

Thanks Dad,

Reg

CHAPTER 10

—James E. Harris
"I refused to become a statistic...
I know what it feels like to be hungry and homeless
due to the lack of a father and a mother."

Background

I was born in 1986 in Richmond, Virginia, and have lived in every part of the city, including North Side, East Side, and West End. My parents were married, and we all lived together. My father was significantly older than my mother. There was a lot of crime; however, there were tight bonds forged within the surrounding communities. My father died when I was five years old and three years later, my mother became terribly ill. This resulted in my younger brother, my baby sister and I becoming wards of the state resulting in us being sent to foster homes. My brother, Tomar is one and a half years younger than me, and my sister, Kierra is three years younger than me, and my sister, Kierra is 3 years younger than me.

My father worked at a hospital however, I am not sure in what compacity. Additionally, he was a handy man in the neighborhood, helping others by doing odd jobs around their houses. My mother did not work. She developed epilepsy and suffered from strokes. This resulted in her being disabled. Growing up, my mother had nurses tending to her around-the-clock. One time, a nurse did not come, and my mother had a seizure. My siblings and I were not picked up from school. This was how social services became involved, and we were removed from the home. They considered the sporadic seizures dangerous to our well-being.

Foster Care vs. Group Home

Each foster care setting was different. Initially, we were in a foster home with an actual mother and father. In addition to my siblings and I, three other children lived within the home at that time. However, the husband and wife became addicted to drugs. The State intervened again, separating my siblings from me. While I never saw my foster parents using drugs, I noticed significant changes in their weight, and attitudes toward each other. There were also some financial challenges due to their abusive drug use.

We were at school when we were taken out of the foster home. I learned that my brother, sister, and myself would be sent to three separate group homes. I did not feel bad for myself. I felt bad for them. The following week, they let us see each other. We hugged. We talked. We cried. We collectively felt a deep seeded resentment towards our foster parents. They failed us. The State entrusted them to care for us, and they were negligent, irresponsible and drug addicted.

Relationship with Siblings

My primary focus became the health and well-being of my siblings. I wanted to make sure they were safe and healthy. I worked at a local grocery store and went to military school, a choice I made because we had to wear uniforms and I no longer had to worry about buying clothes. I used the money I earned to ensure my siblings had everything they needed. I wanted to display and model a certain behavior for my younger siblings to look up to and emulate.

I was fortunate to have a positive relationship with the adults in my siblings' group homes. Unfortunately, my brother's group home had some challenges and were not as progressive as my sister's home or mine. After I left school, I worked to make sure their needs were met, beyond what the State of Virginia provided. We did not attend the same schools which added to the difficulty of caring for my siblings.

When we were young, I helped get them dressed for school. I helped my mother cook. I felt a sense of responsibility to my younger siblings. When we went to separate group homes, I was never given the opportunity to say goodbye. We attended different schools. We asked if we could be together. However, at that time, they denied our request which really weighed heavy on me because I was their protector. To this day, I cannot understand why they would not at least let me stay with my brother. As a result, I now sit on the panel for Rescue Social Services to advocate for children with similar situations.

My brother shares the same ambition as me; however, for the wrong reasons. He became involved in illegal activities. As a result of his actions, he is currently incarcerated. Now, at 32, he has been in and out of prison for more than half his life, for illegal activities including possession of drugs, weapons, and the amount of product he sold. My brother has three children, two girls and a boy from two different women. The children live with their mothers.

Luckily, my sister made better decisions and has never been incarcerated. She works at a call center. She has two little girls. I enjoy the time I spend with my nieces and nephews and love watching the relationship they are building with my daughter. I strongly believe that the way my siblings and I were all affected by our different journeys was a direct result of the absence of our father. Our father's protection would have brought stability, consistency, and structure to our lives which we needed during our early years. I truly believe it would have made the difference for all of us but especially for my brother. As adults, my siblings and I communicate every few days.

Emotional Well-Being

Overall, my experiences in the group home were more positive than negative. However, I was incredibly sad because I missed my siblings. Now that I am a mental health clinician, and can identify the characteristics of depression, I realize that I was not depressed. I found myself just overcompensating, trying to overcome my sister's and my brother's barriers while facing my own.

Extended Family Connections

To my knowledge, my mother had 19 siblings and my father had 21 siblings. I am not sure why the three of us were not placed with one of them. No one seemed willing to step up and lend a hand. I am not sure what this means regarding family and relationships. It used to bother me; however, I have learned to cope with the lack of family support. I never inquired further, as I never found a need to want to know. At that time, I figured they just had their own families and were too busy to take us into their homes. I do not know. To my knowledge, none of my aunts and uncles reached out. We all lived in the same area. Today, there is no relationship with those who are still alive. I know a couple of them, on a superficial level at best. If I walked past most of them, I would not know or recognize them. They now know me, because of my positive impact in the city. I have never tried to reach out to them. For me, it is too late. I am often involved with events in the city helping families in need. On occasion, people approach me saying "I am your cousin on your mom's side or dad's side." At 34 years old, I do not really need new people in my life. It is a tricky situation for me. I have never attempted any searches or tried to connect with my biological family lineage. There is no connection and I have never tried to foster those relationships.

Challenges

I would say I display considerable resilience and tenacity to overcome obstacles. I was blessed and fortunate to be placed in a situation to overcome challenges, and not be dependent on parents. While many people may not understand why I am grateful for the experiences I had in foster care, I know that, at least in those situations, I had a roof over my head and decent food to eat, which, at that time was more than my biological parents could provide for me. I did not see my parents struggle, as I was removed from the household when my mother became ill and by that time my father had already died. From what I know about my father, he was a strong-minded, entrepreneur, always helping people.

I do not recall any challenges in my home with my biological parents. Similarly, I do not recall any challenges in the group home. It was a positive experience for me. At any given time, there were between eight to ten males, and I believe a two to four staff ratio. It was a surprisingly valuable experience. Sometimes, we all got along; and other times, egos would clash. During those rough times, I removed myself from the situation. I always aimed to stay out of trouble with the residents and staff.

It was clear who worked at the group home for a paycheck and who was there to make an impact. Mr. Rodney Hindshell was there to make an impact on our lives. He saw something in me. He pushed me to become the man I am today by always imparting wisdom and mentorship. I thank him for the years he spent encouraging and uplifting me. Those years in the group home, had some extreme highs and lows, but he always found a way to lift our spirits.

Emancipation

Since I was a ward of the State, the State could relinquish rights back to me. The social worker in charge of my case was reluctant to do so because I was a young black male. I did not feel like the system was conducive for growing and developing my dreams and aspirations. I was young, stubborn, and thought I knew it all. I refused to become a statistic. At the age of 16, I was informed that I could emancipate myself which meant that I would be considered a legal adult. After learning this, I asked a friend of a friend to go to court with me and support me in this endeavor. This request was granted which was the beginning of my journey into adulthood.

I was fortunate enough to be able to take care of myself but every day was not a good day. I worked and had a car but many times I had to sleep in hotel rooms or at friend's houses. I had to make decisions that most 16-year-olds never have to make. I could even sign my own notes for school trips. I just made it work! Because it was not all good, those experiences made me work harder. I know what it feels like to be hungry and homeless!

Family

In 2012, I married my daughter's mother. Unfortunately, we grew apart. While I was set on entrepreneurship, she feared it. She listened to people outside of our marriage. While I was overseas in 2014, she left; and in 2016, we divorced. I have no regrets. I would rather we be separate and happy, as opposed to my daughter growing up in a toxic environment with a skewed and inaccurate view of marriage.

I do not believe family can be compartmentalized into "normal" and/or "abnormal." I believe each family is an entity of its own. Happiness is self-constructed. No one should remain in a toxic relationship, as they supply no positive benefit for a family.

My daughter, Peyton is 8 years old. She is smart, charismatic, ambitious, and open. She splits her time between her mother and me. We co-parent. She has accompanied me to several local events. She is involved in the Waffle Diner and the Art Gallery. In fact, the LLC for my business is her name. Also, she knows about the mental health movement. She is wonderful. When my daughter is an adult, I want her to be with a man she can be free with, one who is nurturing and supportive; one who expresses himself in positive ways that she understands.

Education

Military school was great during my years in high school. It was a small school, no more than 300 students. For the most part, I excelled, as I was able to obtain many accommodations, lead drill teams and won local and national awards. There was a true sense of pride, setting a good example, learning different disciplines and being in an environment that was different than I am accustomed. I was fortunate to have had such a positive high school experience. To this day, I am still close with everyone who attended school with me.

While in high school, I was on the drill team, the saber team, and the marksmanship team. I also had a job. Holding leadership positions in high school fostered my ability to remain focused and driven. When I decided to emancipate myself, I felt prepared to take on life's journey, because of high school, I had grown within myself, gained leadership potential, willingness, drive, and ambition to want to set a positive example for my community. I graduated in the top ten of my graduating class.

When I initially enrolled in college, I attended St. Paul's College. However, I then enrolled in the military and was deployed in my sophomore year. St. Paul closed soon after. It was one of the oldest historically black colleges and universities (HBCU) in the country but had to close after 125 years due to a host of problems, including losing funding. When I returned home, I transferred to another university. I graduated with my bachelor's degree in Clinical Psychology, and my master's degree in Clinical and Mental Counseling from South University.

Career

Being an entrepreneur was always my passion. Often, I was off on my own, deep into my own creativity, and growing within myself. At the age of 12 years old, I began working at a grocery store, pulling carts, helping people with bags, etc.

Currently, I am a serial entrepreneur, multi-entrepreneur, multi-homeowner. I own four properties, three businesses and 16 investments between North Carolina, Virginia, and the D.C. area. While I was on a two week leave from my first tour, I started the process of building my first property. I joined the military because I was homeless; I needed to eat. Two months after finishing my tour, my home was move-in ready. At 22, I was a homeowner. From there, my hunger was insatiable. My home is in Columbia Heights, around the corner from Virginia State University in Petersburg, Va. Less than 10 miles from Fort Lee Military Base. I strategically built the house in this location, knowing that I could rent it to a college student or military family. This was my first business venture. I continued working and saving money, being financially conscious and literate.

Sometime after beginning my investing business, I bought a car. By chance, I met a man who schooled me on purchasing a rental property, having tenants pay me, and making money. After that meeting, I learned how to sew income and have enough for a down payment for my next house. Tenants rented the house. The mortgage on the house was less than the car. I traded in the car and purchased one that was more financially practical. Since then, I purchased two additional properties, for a total of four properties.

During my next deployment, a friend was looking for an investor in a coffee shop. I became the primary investor in that business venture. I also started a carpet cleaning company (Royal Carpet Care), so my brother could have a job. I oversaw all logistical components (such as marketing, buying a van, etc.) and my brother was going to clean the carpets. I marketed the company as Military Black owned. Unfortunately, my brother was arrested right before we launched the business. For about two years, I worked at this company before and after my regular job as a teacher's assistant at an alternative school. Eventually, I was able to hire people to work for me. I later sold the carpet cleaning company.

I was looking to buy a Porsche but purchased a party bus instead and began another business venture. I had this company in service for about two years. We drove large groups to weddings, proms, and trips to the MGM Casino in Maryland. Once the insurance drastically increased, I sold it to a youth organization.

I have a waffle diner called Grill's Waffle in Richmond, Virginia. I also have an Art Gallery, which hosts art events for the city, open, mic nights, paintings, and poetry nights. It is helpful for people in the city to sell their artwork. At the Healing Hub we service clients with outpatient therapy, Zumba, yoga, sessions for first time home buying, credit repair, and restoration rights. Prior to the COVID pandemic, we would feed and give clothes to the less fortunate.

In April, I became an author. My book is titled "Man Just Express Yourself!: An Interactive Guide for MEN, Young and Old." The book discusses goals, trauma, depression, misogyny, different topics men typically avoid discussing because of societal stigmas. As a therapist, I want to break the barriers and remove the humiliation. To date, I have sold about 1,000 books.

Two years ago, I started a movement called Men to Heal, which focuses on male mental and physical health. I have spoken in many states and countries across the globe. Public speaking is a big part of our program – speaking about men's overall wellness, discussing different diagnosis, the importance of early detection and regular prostate exams. Heart disease is the number one killer of Black men – so we strongly encourage men to get physicals, go to the doctor, and learn to comfortably display emotions and affection toward others. I have learned that men all over the world are having the same issues and concerns. I met a young woman in Columbia who said that the men there have "cheesmo" effect, which is equivalent to the male ego. Men are expected to be macho and display certain qualities. These are characteristics we work to identify and lessen.

I hear that my father was enterprising. I am not sure how much my parents affected my desire to succeed. I do know that being in the group home and being homeless made me want more, not only for myself but also for others. I feel these experiences were vital in developing my ambition and passion for giving. But, if I lived with my parents, it is unlikely that I would have gone to military school. I would have gone to the neighborhood school, played sports, and gone straight to college.

Struggles

I never want to experience homelessness and hunger again. I would never want my daughter to experience it. After I graduated high school, I attended St. Paul's College. During breaks, I would sneak back in the dorm. I would leave something in the window, so I could get back in the building; my room was on the first floor. I would stay on campus, while everyone was on break. I had my microwave in the car. I would go to the store to get meat to make sandwiches, Hot Pockets, and other food to eat. One of the old workers (Rodney Hindshell) from the group home found out what I was doing to survive. His son had just moved out of state with his mother. He told me I could just stay with him on breaks. To make ends meet, I was selling snacks, warming up people's food out of my car's microwave, drafting college essays, driving people to stores, doing homework – hustling! This influenced my decision to join the army in my sophomore year.

I coped with the division in the family by trying to excel. I focused on my passion and being above my current situation. At that time, my current situation was living in the group home. I vividly remember creating a vision board. I had houses, different business and (pretty much) everything I have now. Two weeks after creating this vision board, I emancipated myself. I focused on this, setting a good example for my siblings, and providing for them in every way possible. I had a kind circle of friends who would let me crash on their couch and Mr. Rodney Hindshell who let me sleep in his son's room. Because of my dedicated support system, I was able to focus on where I wanted to go and how I would get there.

Military

When I went to the Army, I experienced an intense feeling of grief. I was there so I could eat and care for my family. When you are in basic training, they have film crews who record soldiers who stand out and excel. In my unit, I was that person, partially because I attended a military school, so I was familiar with some basics, and because I was hungry. Not only in the literal sense but I wanted to succeed so I had something to send home to my siblings. I was fortunate to grow from that situation.

I served eight years in the army with two deployments, one in Iraq and one in Afghanistan. During both tours, I served as a combat engineering, gunner, lead husky driver. My first tour in Iraq was almost two years. The mission was to clear the routes for the additional log packs who bring food, supplies and logistical items. The tours were graphic, severe. There were explosions, gun fights. We burst out and did road clearance. Our job was to locate the Infrared Explosive Devices (IEDs). Between 2007-2008, Iraq wanted all US troops out by a certain time. The US government did not allow us to leave, and the results were catastrophic. We were hit left and right. Our missions increased from 12 hours to 16-18 hours per day. We would talk, laugh, joke and many times cry. We would be coming in from a shift and another team would be leaving for a shift, and someone would not come back. It was so deadly; gun fires and explosions increased. In many cases, we lost people. We lost four people on my first tour, one who was a close friend. It was a hard tour. It was also fun, needed and helped me to develop significantly. I was happy to be part of a group and have so much comradery. It was so passionate. If we did not protect each other, we could have been the one who did not return from a shift. There were many good times, and miserable times, losing members of our team.

Nothing can prepare a person who must witness first-hand the loss of a team member. You can rise to your level of training or sink to your level of training. I was fortunate enough not to see anyone killed in front of me. I saw significant bloodshed during my tours, but not deaths. Other people that I was close to serving in other platoons died, but not in ours. What was also difficult was the heat. Iraq was 137 degrees with the heat index, with our uniforms on. This made our assignments extremely uncomfortable, but we always made it work, without complaints.

Influences

Sgt. Thornton was a military veteran teacher. He would tell you if your work was not academically or behaviorally acceptable. He would tell you his opinion of your potential, and that could be presented in a stern manner, like "Yo, what the hell are you doing? This is not you. Don't do that." Or he could be passive, "You have to set the example." Thorton, as well as some of the other teachers knew my story. They did not allow that to prevent me from doing what was expected. Having them as leaders and mentors ensured that I would stay the course. I had a responsibility to maintain certain levels, to ensure my ranks were not removed.

Wanting people to see a better world influences my passion to become a better person. I want everyone to win. I want to leave my legacy for my daughter. I want her to understand what a gentleman is and how he should express himself. I want to live what I say. I can tell her what to do all day long. Living is how we develop our children. If I show her what to do and model what to do, she will gravitate toward this way of life.

I look at people who have overcome obstacles, whether they were traumatic or required increased tenacity. I just recently watched the *Living Chronicles of Master P*. He has always been one of my favorite entrepreneur celebrities. Kobe Bryant is also one of my favorites. I wanted to author a book about both and the work-ethic they possessed. You hear about Master P having to overcome so many obstacles, such as living in the projects. For me that was gratifying to learn about, as I could relate to the experience. You would hear Kobe's teammates saying he was practicing two hours before the team, eight hours with the team and stayed after the team's practice. That emulates a magnificent work ethic and I want to work with more people like him/them. Their stories resonate with me. I am at the point in my life where I want to predominately associate myself with others who share this same mindset.

My life's message:

Have ambition.

Have tenacity.

Do not count yourself out like the world is going to try to count you out.

Be focused and driven on what you plan to do.

You are your only limit! You can only limit yourself!

Create a plan.

Work and implement the plan.

Be authentic.

If you give someone the ability to feed you, they can have the same ability to starve you.

Create your own!

Letter to Dad

Dear Dad,

I wish we had more time. I wish I would have been fortunate enough to know you, and hear more about you, as far as what you had done. I hope you are proud of me. I hope I am walking in the legacy you extended. I hope you are watching over me...

Love James

CHAPTER 11

—*Bryan Dearry*
*"After my father passed away, family members thought
I was going to go off the deep end."*

Childhood Experiences

I am from the great city of Philadelphia. I have always lived in Philadelphia, I was born and raised here. I am from the gritty area of Logan, a section of North Philadelphia. I was born in Germantown Hospital; my mother was 32 and my father four years older.

My mother is from Detroit, MI. My father is from South Carolina. My parents were both raised in large families. My mother is the eldest of her family and has seven younger sisters. My mother was raised by her grandmother, separately from her siblings. I remember my great-grandmother. She was stern, yet extremely loving. At times she watched me as a child when my parents were working. My mother was a nurse who helped deliver babies, and often had to work overnight shifts.

My father had six brothers and three sisters. Many remark that I look like my father. My mother tells me I look like my father when he was my age, tall, dark complexion, beard, and physique. I believe I have some of my mother's facial features, such as her nose but mostly I think I look more like my father.

My parents met by chance, as my father's friend and my maternal grandmother lived across the street from each other. My mother lived with her grandmother and while my father was visiting his friend, they met. Even though they attended separate high schools, they were high school sweethearts, married for 19 years. My parents' marriage provided an illustration for me that people can be married, happy, and raise a family together. It felt like we were one of the families you see on television. We ate dinner as a family. To this day, I have never heard my mother speak negatively of my father, and when he was alive, my father always spoke positively about my mother.

My parents tried to provide me and my brother more than they had when they were growing up. I believe my parents' upbringing had a direct impact on how we were raised. As I grew older, I learned details about situations with my mother's childhood that gave me insight about why I experienced certain feelings as a child. My mother has a different father from her siblings. As a result, she was not raised in the same house as her siblings but down the street with her grandmother. At times, I feel that my mother rejected me. There is no blueprint to parenting, and I was putting her through so much. At the time, I may have internalized it as rejection. Now that I am older, I see it differently.

My mother was the disciplinarian in the house, which contributed to our strife. My father had a different approach to discipline. His tone differed from my mother's and I had more respect for him. We had a different relationship. My mother was a nurse and often worked overnight, leaving my father and I together often. My father taught me how to ride a bike, tie a tie, and did homework with my brother and me. He was hands on. We had time to nourish and develop a relationship. My father was the fun parent, the parent you could talk to; we would play cards, and at times kids from the neighborhood would come over to play cards with us, but really it was to play with him. My mother was the dictator. My mother went to Catholic school, which I believe contributed to her stringent demeanor, including elevated expectations, and a demanding, rigorous work ethic. While I despised those characteristics then, I now embody them as positive attributes, intricately woven into the man I have become.

Adolescent – Tough Times

Growing up, I was rambunctious, a jokester, sarcastic, and always talking back to adults. I was kicked out of school in both fourth and fifth grade. I was written up, given detention, and suspended, both in and out of school. I was always in trouble, using inappropriate, vulgar language toward my teachers and classmates. I was hanging with the wrong crowd and truant from school. By the time I was in the sixth grade, I found myself in family court, facing the repercussions of my actions.

Looking back at that time, I was a lost boy, living day to day. I could not see a future for myself. What I valued and what was best for me were not the same. My friend's opinions mattered most. While in middle school I became engaged in fighting, defiance and situations that are not becoming of anyone, especially a young Black man. I started trouble in the community, smoking marijuana and going against any level of authority.

I had no real direction and was easily manipulated by the wrong individuals because, at that time, I had no love for myself. I had no self-worth; I was fighting, jumping people, cutting school, smoking marijuana, drinking – all the behaviors of a misguided person. When I was in middle school, the school uniform policies in Philadelphia were identical across the city. There was no way to identify what school students attended based on uniform. My friends and I felt this worked in our favor and we would cut school, go to another school, run through the hallways, pulling fire alarms, and laughing as school police chased us. I found myself spending far too much time with people older than me, giving me access to many situations that I truly regretted.

Because I found myself in trouble all the time (both in and out of school), my parents sent me for counseling. My mischievous behavior caused my mother significant stress and anxiety. It was a major contributor to the dysfunction in our relationship. As I got older, my mother's attitude toward me started to change. When I was younger, I thought my mother did not like me. We rarely engaged in small talk. After the passing of my father, life shifted drastically. I guess this was where our relationship started to avalanche out of control. This diminished our ability to communicate effectively. I admit, this was my fault, I was a lot to handle. Consequences had no impact on me; she was not going to physically discipline me and a loss of privileges meant nothing. I think my mother felt as though she was going to lose me to the temptation of the streets.

8th Grade Graduation

I doubt my mother believed I would complete eighth grade. I feel so grateful that my father was able to see me graduate from eighth grade- it was monumental. I feel like this was truly a time when my parents were proud of me – the looks on their faces. Although my actions did not show it, I wanted to make my parents proud. This time, they were at the school to see me walk across the stage – after achieving my academic requirements. Unfortunately, this was the last graduation my father would see, but was not my last.

My Father's Death

My father passed away from a heart attack at 50 years old. Prior to the heart attack, he suffered several strokes. I remember him needing a wheelchair. The day my father passed is still quite vivid for me. It was summertime. I was in basketball camp. I was walking to the store with my friends. My God-sister and a family friend appeared, telling me they were picking me up. I asked why? They took me to the hospital. My Godfather was crying; no one would tell me what was wrong. I felt in my spirit that something was wrong. My mother confirmed my thoughts. Everyone was crying. I felt my father's cold lifeless body lying on the table.

How? How was this possible? This had to be a nightmare. I had just seen my father that morning. Seeing my father like that was devastating. The night before, I was disrespectful towards my mother. My father verbally disciplined me. I was annoyed by something he said so I did not speak to him before I left the house the next day. I never got to speak with him again. This shook me to my core. This was all happening too fast, and I felt as though I did not have enough time to process all I was thinking and feeling. I still have not forgiven myself for not speaking to him that morning. However, I have attempted to deal with the emotions, and at times I feel better. For a long time, I thought I stressed him out, and was responsible. If I had a chance to do it all over again, I would speak to my father, give him the traditional, "I love you, Dad" and give him a hug.

After that, the mood in the house was absent, lifeless. Family dinners disappeared. We stopped watching tv together. We stopped sitting at the table doing homework. My mother felt overwhelmed. There was no one there to do all my father did for us. It was like a house full of zombies. It was never the same. My father's passing made me aware of death. Life is something worth cherishing because you do not know when people are going to die. It made me become more responsible. It changed me in a sense that I am reluctant, even fearful to want to love someone on that level, knowing they will die someday. I do not want to open old wounds and feel that type of pain again. I have built protective emotional walls around myself.

As an adult, I feel like I need my father more now than ever. I could have used his advice about getting my first home, females, parenting, being a man in the city. I need him to bounce ideas off and for him to be my sounding board. Initially, I was sad. That sadness blossomed into anger. I was angry about my father dying. I feel like he was a good person. There are so many bad people in the world. My father did not deserve to die. I was extremely angry. Unfortunately, I still have not dealt with that anger. It is easier to run away from the situation rather than work through the pain. I know this is hindering me, but I am just not ready. In all honesty, not dealing with it is how I have been dealing with it.

Coping

My coping mechanism was running away, smoking weed, using alcohol, socializing with my friends. I was painting a façade of a reality that was non-existent. I wanted to reflect on my father as little as possible. At one point, I was running away from the memories, trying to delete them by getting high. Another coping strategy was shutting down – isolating myself from others.

I still use some of these strategies today. While they might not be beneficial for everyone, they work for me. I would not recommend them to others.

I went to counseling after my father passed away. It was not beneficial, because I was reluctant to share my feelings with the therapist. It felt unnatural. I had a history with counseling, having tried it twice before. For me, talking about past events and emotions did not change the outcome. I did not want to deal with the emotions I was feeling.

A Mentor When I Needed One the Most

I was closer to my father than my mother which made life extremely difficult after he passed. Fortunately, my family was rooted in the church which became part of our extended family. There was a family in particular, Alphonso and Tamika Evans, that were truly an intercession for me in my life. After my dad's passing, Alphonso saw something in me, and began mentoring me. I am not sure if my mother had a part in making the connection with the Evans' at that time, but if she was, I am grateful she did. After my father died, my mother and I had a strained relationship. Alphonso became the sounding board I needed, a valuable resource in providing wide-ranging advice. Our relationship has now blossomed into a father-son relationship. He supplies more than mentorship; he offers guidance, love, and something intangible that every child needs. He tells me things I do not want but need to hear, helping prevent and/or mend events both past and present. I am not perfect, but Alphonso's guidance helped me become the man I am today. I do not know if I would even be here were it not for the love and sacrifices that he and his family have given me.

Through Alphonso's mentorship, my sense of uncertainty was finally addressed. My relationship with Alphonso helped mold me because he offered insight that was unique to what I had received in the past. He challenged me to love myself, a concept I had never even considered prior to meeting him. He loved me, even when I did not love myself. I think this is how our relationship developed. I asked him, "Why did you choose me?" There were so many other young people in the church who needed a mentor. He reminded me that he could see the greatness within me and that he knew I was in a space to be mentored and just needed someone to help navigate me through some trying times of growing up. He believed in me.

I am forever indebted to him and his family; our relationship developed so naturally. They assisted in raising me before they even had children of their own. I have been a part of their family for a long time. Alphonso pushed me, called me out when I was wrong, made me acknowledge the way I treated my mother, and provided feedback on my good and bad choices in life. He taught me how to drive, drove to my college, met with my teachers regarding academic and behavioral concerns, and shared with me countless, invaluable, life lessons. I learned to always have faith in God, finish what I start and to remember the importance of a family, even if not connected through blood. Not everyone is blessed with a loving supportive family. I feel so fortunate they showed me love and provided a foundation I needed to grow and develop.

Church was Home

My family has strong connections to our family church – Tenth Memorial Baptist Church, located in North Philadelphia. My father grew up in this church, my parents were married in this church and my father's funeral was in this church. This is the church where I met Alphonso. I grew up in my church. I served on the Usher Board with Alphonso's wife,

Tamika. I was in the church choir. The church offered youth Bible study, so we could have some positive activities and Tamika was one of the teachers who would talk to us, encouraging us to remain grounded and faithful to God.

For me, church was beneficial because there were a lot of people my age who attended our church. I was never bored in church because of the large youth focus. This made me want to be there. When I was growing up, church was not a cool thing however, seeing other youth in the church made me want to attend. The activities were engaging and I made some of my life-long friends at church. My upbringing in the church instilled many positive lessons. While I am not an active member, I still consider the members my family. When I see church members in public, I know they love, pray, embrace and encourage me.

I do not go to church anymore because of my internal struggles. When I was a child, my mother made me go to church. I am more appreciative of that now. My life could be so different. I am grateful for people who have planted seeds in me, prayed over those seeds, and have been there to see growth and development. Some of my friends did not have those kind of prayer warriors or loving people in their corner to support them. The world can be a cold, wicked place. Church definitely played a major role in my life even when I could not appreciate its role.

Family Relationships

Relationships with my family members are extreme. My relationship with my immediate family is not ideal. We do not speak as much as I would hope. These atypical norms formed early in my childhood. I love my mother, but I have come to accept certain things will never occur in our relationship. I saw other people's relationships and wanted that for me and my mom. I had to come to the realization that this will never be our relationship, but it does not mean we cannot have a relationship. I try to understand that our relationship is unique, and that each parent/child relationship is different. Over the years, my relationship with my mother has improved. But it is still not where I would like it to be.

I also have a strained relationship with my brother. I love him tremendously. We do not speak to each other, and to be honest, I do not even know why. I carry guilt with the lack of communication that exists between us. When my brother needed me, I was not there for him. As he was getting older, I should have taken more time with him, but I focused on myself and my needs. When our father died, I became selfish and was causing my family more harm than good. This took away attention that my brother needed. Everyone focused on my nonsense and no one checked on him. I never even asked him, "How are you dealing with daddy's death?" I can see the damage now and wish there was a way to mend this relationship.

One day, I hope to have a family of my own. I want them to embrace my mother and brother and want my mother and brother to embrace them. When I think of my current relationship with my mother and brother I do not know if this will be possible. I do know that this will not be the type of relationship I have with my children.

Struggles

When I was young, I do not remember ever seeing my mother struggle. She was never vocal about it with me. She was always on the move, raising her two sons and working. I think this helped keep her mind from thinking about her loss and heartache. As I got older, my mother started showing signs of depression. Life was not the same. The house that was always clean began to show signs of disarray. She used to be more vibrant and active but with time, she would arrive home and head straight to her bedroom. I was too selfish to notice. When I was finally able to see the struggles of others, I came to the realization that I was not the only one who had lost someone. She lost her husband and life-long friend.

College Years

My college years were phenomenal. I met people from different backgrounds. I attended Virginia State University (VSU), receiving my bachelor's degree in Mass Communication, with a concentration in television and radio. VSU is an HBCU located in Petersburg, VA. I learned so much about myself and my rich history as an African American. I was exposed to a world I never knew existed. College opened my mind and forced me to grow up. It humbled me. Initially, college was a culture shock. It was in a rural area. I did not know I was afraid of the dark until I went to college. Growing up in the city, it was never completely dark – streetlights, ambient sounds from people walking down the street, cars, etc. In Petersburg, it gets pitch black – no streetlights. It is so dark; you could not see your hand in front of your face. Additionally, there is no sound. Just you, living in your own silence. It was an adjustment.

People were friendlier in the South. Growing up in Philadelphia, there is more aggression, and life moves at a faster pace. I learned to slow down in the South. People use manners and are polite. Men open and hold the doors for ladies and other men. I met people who changed my perspective about life and about myself. I learned about my heritage. Growing up I only saw negative images of Africa; impoverished, malnourished communities. I had no idea that Africa has complex skyscrapers. Some of the richest countries are in Africa. A lot of our exports are from Africa. It is not just the place where slaves came from, people starving, and dying of AIDS, as depicted in many American outlets. It is a vibrant continent, full of resources and people who speak many languages. College exposed me to this type of education.

Now, I have a master's degree in Early Childhood and Special Education. Receiving my master's was my third graduation that I did not see my dad in the audience looking proud. I always felt something was missing at high school and college graduations, because my father had died. Other people being at those ceremonies were kind but did not mean as much, because the person I wanted to be there most, was not.

Favorite Teacher

Mr. Reading was my favorite teacher. He was a black man. He made school fun, engaging and not foreign. He taught geometry in a way that was entertaining, and he was patient. He would work with you, after school if necessary. To this day, he stays connected with his former students. He always gave us positive affirmations. He would correct us using a positive tone. He made us want to go to class. I cut other classes, but not his, because I wanted to be there.

Currently, I am an elementary school teacher. I have taught kindergarten and now teach third grade. I try to be empathic and relatable to my students. I try to be understanding of their needs and engage them like Mr. Reading did for me. I want my students to value education and not feel lost. I want them to focus on being children.

Letter to Dad

Dear Dad, I love you. I miss you. I hope I am making you proud.

Bryan

FINAL THOUGHTS

I am reminded of a popular biblical reference from 1st Thessalonians 5:17 and 5:18 where it states, "Pray without ceasing. In everything give thanks: for this is the will of God in Christ Jesus concerning you" (KJV).

Many of the book contributor's personal stories are stories full of life lessons, some regrets, and some successes. As sons who grew into strong men, many of the book's contributors turned tragedies into triumphs. Conversely, as many of them continue to navigate their manhood by protecting their families and negotiating their life circumstances, they have the hope and desire to succeed in an ever-changing society filled with setbacks. Other contributors have been able to transfer that positive energy of their father-son experiences to impact the lives of many generations. It is important to also note that within everyone's chapter, they were able to become successful college graduates, excelling in their respected fields of human endeavor. This strength speaks to the determination, grit, and perseverance of one to achieve; in many cases, against all odds; against disfunction, some more than others; and against some heartache and pain regarding their fathers.

As we continue to embark upon various nuances within our life, there is a constant within the core family, "Dads." While mothers are often celebrated, "Dads" are often overlooked. Understanding the diverse needs of fathers and sons and/or daughters may still be a novelty, but with the willingness to do the work, one can better understand their father and how to embrace a frequently "complex" human being. Love, forgiveness, peace, and the ability to give thanks in every situation is exercised when you truly take the risk to meet your father. Romans 8:28 states, "And we know that all things work together for good to them that love God, to them who are the called according to his purpose (KJV)."

As I matriculate, the life lessons of my ancestors ferociously resonate with me, encouraging me to continue loving, giving thanks and appreciating life's good, bad and ugly, because it shapes, and continues to shape, the culture, minds, systems, procedures, and life I live today.

In closing, young men and women, remember that greatness is among you! Your dreams, desires and detours will make you fierce competitors in this ever-changing world. You will develop a knack to help others with your stories of forgiveness, love, and trust if you understand these concepts. As you continue to navigate this experience called, "life," remember that you are not alone. Someone has gone through a similar obstacle, experienced similar emotions, and has overcome love, pain, abuse, cruelty, peace, prosperity, and even discrimination. Know that God loves you and so does your village, and yes, so does your father!

To share your stories of father-son or father-daughter relationships or simply stories of life-lessons navigating the presence or lack of a father in your life, feel free to contact me at www.DrAlphonsoEvans.com

Dad, is that you?

For some of us, we can remember those big hands over our little ones from the beginning,

For some of us, we knew that clear distinctive difference in the tone when you said, come here man!

For some of us, we would listen for a certain walk or the way a door closed to say,

Dad, is that you?

For some of us, you were the first name we called.

For some of us, we could not wait until you uttered those famous words, "This is my son."

For some of us, you were the only real superhero.

Dad is that you?

For some of us, you never existed.

For some of us, we could hear and see the fights with the female version

For some of us, you walked away and, in some cases, never came back.

Dad is that you?

For some of us, we still can smell your cologne even though you left the streets of concrete forever.

For some of us, we sit and wonder what would have been different if you were here.

For some of us, we cry on the inside in order to make you proud of the man we have become.

Dad is that you?

For some of us, the bond was one of the best experiences ever that we want to recreate for the next generation.

For some of us, the bond never had the other half to be mended which has created a lost generation.

But no matter our experience with you, rather we are smiling at your legacy or grieving because of your absence.

We still love you and are reminded every time we look back at ourselves that we are only here because of you.

Dad is that you?

-------Dr. Alphonso Evans Sr.

I am excited about Dr. Alphonso Evans's sophomore book entitled, "Taking the Risk… Meet Your Father".

With the ever-changing landscape of "father-son", "father-daughter" relationships, this book is sure to give insight on evolving relationships, or even the lack thereof within our communities. Hopefully, this work will bring meaningful intellectual discourse on what must be done to enhance fundamental relationships amongst fathers' and their children.

As I reflect on my own father and my relationship with him growing up; one thing is for sure, MY FATHER IS MY HERO!!! I am a product of the old proverb, "It takes a village to raise a child", and he's ensured my village is strong. These experiences I write about in my own New York Times Bestselling book, "My Vanishing Country: A Memoir".

To that end, I have been blessed to have three children of my own; one son and two daughters, who are abundantly loved. I hope to continue to foster a village for all of my children throughout their lives, as I strive to become the HERO to them my father has been and continues to be for me. Furthermore, I am privileged to share so many experiences with my children. Regardless of events, my work or otherwise; I always make time for them.

Enjoy reading Dr. Alphonso Evans' sophomore book entitled, "Taking the Risk… Meet Your Father".

—Bakari Sellers